BOOKS EVERY CHILD
SHOULD KNOW

BOOKS EVERY CHILD SHOULD KNOW

The Literature Quiz Book

Nancy Polette

LIBRARIES UNLIMITED

A Member of the Greenwood Publishing Group

Westport, Connecticut · London

Library of Congress Cataloging-in-Publication Data

Polette, Nancy.
   Books every child should know: the literature quiz book / by Nancy Polette.
      p.   cm
   Includes bibliographical references.
   ISBN: 1-59158-354-3 (pbk. : alk. paper)
      1. Children's libraries—Activity programs. 2. School libraries—Activity programs.
   3. Reading promotion. 4. Children's literature—Study and teaching (Elementary)—
   Activity programs. 5. Tales—Study and teaching (Elementary)—Activity programs.
   6. Creative activities and seat work. I. Title.
   Z718.1.P74   2006
   027.62'5—dc22   2005030841

British Library Cataloguing in Publication Data is available.

Library of Congress Catalog Card Number: 2005030841
ISBN: 1-59158-354-3

First published in 2006

Libraries Unlimited, 88 Post Road West, Westport, CT 06881
A Member of the Greenwood Publishing Group, Inc.
www.lu.com

Printed in the United States of America

The paper used in this book complies with the
Permanent Paper Standard issued by the National
Information Standards Organization (Z39.48–1984).

10   9   8   7   6   5   4   3   2

CONTENTS

INTRODUCTION

The *Literature Quiz Book* has three purposes:

1. To turn quizzes into fun games that allow children to enjoy the experience of literature.

2. To promote children's fluency through the reading of books and stories in a wide variety of genres.

3. To assess children's knowledge of literature.

The book is divided into genres so that the parent, teacher, or librarian can integrate the quizzes and games with the study of a wide variety of literature. Quizzes and games are included for Mother Goose rhymes, Aesop's fables, Greek and Roman myths, folktales from Germany, France, Great Britain, Scandinavia, Asia, India, and Africa, as well as Hispanic tales, and Native American tales and fantasy.

Games and quizzes are also included for the classics in children's literature, as well as quizzes and games related to the Newbery and Caldecott Medal Award winners.

Quizzes can be undertaken by individuals, teams, or entire groups. Children will find word searches, cryptograms, library scavenger hunts, stories with hidden titles by favorite authors, and much more. Quizzes should be introduced as games and not as tests. Enough material is included here to conduct a schoolwide Literature Game Bowl.

The *Literature Quiz Book* is designed to help busy teachers and librarians implement either introductory or culminating activities for any genre of literature. the use of the quizzes and games can be as creative as the adult who introduces and uses them.

MOTHER GOOSE RIDDLES

Who blew his horn
because the cow was in the corn?

1._____

Who went to sea
With silver buckles on his knee?

2._____

Hickory dickory dock
Who ran up the clock?

3._____

Who was the pumpkin eater
Who had a wife but couldn't keep
her?

4.

_____

Who fell off a wall?

5._____

Who fell down
and broke his crown?

6._____

One could eat no fat,
One could eat no lean
Who licked the platter clean?

7._____

Who wandered upstairs, downstairs
and in my lady's chamber?

8._____

Who was a merry old soul
with a pipe and a bowl?

9._____

Who was the piper's son
who stole a pig, and away he run?

10._____

Key: 1. Little Boy Blue 2. Bobby Shaftoe 3. mouse 4. Peter 5. Humpty
Dumpty 6. Jack 7. Jack Sprat & his wife 8. Wee Willie Winkle 9. Old King
Cole 10. Tom

MOTHER GOOSE RIDDLE SONGS

Tune: The Bear Went Over the Mountain

1. Who fell off of a high wall
   Who fell off of a high wall
   Who fell off of a high wall
   It's a name that starts with H

   H_____

2. Who lost all of their mittens?
   Who lost all of their mittens?
   Who lost all of their mittens?
   It's a name that starts with K.

   K_____

3. Who jumped over a candlestick?
   Who jumped over a candlestick?
   Who jumped over a candlestick?
   It's a name that starts with J.

   J_____

4. Who was scared by a spider?
   Who was scared by a spider?
   Who was scared by a spider?
   It's a name that starts with M.

   M_____

5. Who lost all of her fluffy sheep?
   Who lost all of her fluffy sheep?
   Who lost all of her fluffy sheep?
   It's a name that starts with B.

   B_____

6. What boy was the piper's son?
   What boy was the piper's son?
   What boy was the piper's son?
   It's a name hat starts with T.

   T_____

7. What did Lucy Locket lose?
   What did Lucy Locket lose?
   What did Lucy Locket lose?
   It's a word that starts with P.

   P_____

8. Where did Old Mother Hubbard go?
   Where did Old Mother Hubbard go?
   Where did Old Mother Hubbard go?
   It's a word that starts with C.

   C_____

Key: Humpty Dumpty 2. 3 kittens 3. Jack 4. Miss Muffet 5. Bo Peep
6. Tom 7. pocket 8. cupboard

MOTHER GOOSE QUIZ

Secret Words

Circle the letter under True if the statement is true.

Circle the letter under False if the statement is false.

Place the circled letters in order on the lines at the bottom of the page to find the secret words.

	TRUE	FALSE
1. Tom was the butcher's son.	L	M
2. Mary was quite contrary.	O	J
3. Miss Muffet was afraid of a bat.	E	T
4. Jack jumped over a river.	S	H
5. Mary had a little lamb.	E	A
6. Old King Cole was happy.	R	N
7. Four men were in a tub.	I	G
8. Five kittens lost their mittens.	S	O
9. Peter, Peter ate apples.	N	O
10. Humpty Dumpty fell off a wall.	S	T
11. Georgie Porgie hit the girls.	D	E

___ ___ ___ ___ ___ ___

___ ___ ___ ___ ___

Secret words: Mother Goose

A MOTHER GOOSE MYSTERY PLAY:
THE CASE OF THE MISSING BOWL

Add the missing words. Read the play. Solve the mystery.

Reading Parts: Narrator; Miss Muffet; Wee Willie Winkie; Tom; the Piper's Son; The Jack of Hearts; Jack Sprat

Miss Muffet: Oh dear, oh dear, oh dear! Someone has taken my cereal bowl. It was my special bowl. I eat cereal only on Sundays. The other days of the week I eat curds and whey.

Wee Willie Winkie: What did your Sunday cereal bowl look like?

Miss Muffet: It was purple with pink spots. My curds and whey bowls are pink with purple spots. I used those at my ice cream party last night.

Wee Willie Winkie: We will ask all the guests if they saw the bowl. Let's visit Tom, the Piper's son, first. He is a prime suspect. Everyone knows that he once stole a **(1)**_____.

Narrator: Miss Muffet and Wee Willie Winkie found Tom alone in a schoolroom writing on a paper.

Wee Willie Winkie: Tom, have you seen Miss Muffet's special Sunday cereal bowl?

Tom: Is that the pink bowl with purple spots? I had a bowl like that full of ice cream last night. I can't talk to you any more. I have to write 100 times I will never again steal a **(2)**_____.

Narrator: On they went to talk to the Jack of Hearts. He was also a thief. He once stole some **(3)**_____.

Wee Willie Winkie: Jack, have you seen Miss Muffet's Sunday cereal bowl?

Jack: Was it pink with purple spots or purple with pink spots? I don't know what bowls she used at her ice cream party last night. I wasn't invited.

Wee Willie Winkie: Maybe Jack Sprat stole your bowl. Every time I peek through their **(4)**_____ they are eating. He eats no **(5)**_____ and she eats no **(6)**_____. Maybe now they are licking your Sunday cereal bowl clean.

Narrator: When Wee Willie Winkie rang their doorbell, Jack Sprat and his wife stopped eating long enough to answer the door.

From Books Every Child Should Know: The Literature Quiz Book by Nancy Polette. Westport, CT: Libraries Unlimited. Copyright © 2006.

Miss Muffet: Have you seen my special Sunday Cereal bowl?

Jack Sprat: What was so special about the bowls you served ice cream in last night? They all were pink with purple spots. I couldn't tell one from another. Besides, I prefer platters to bowls. They hold more food.

Wee Willie Winkie: We don't need to talk to any more suspects. I know who stole your special Sunday cereal bowl. Do you?

Who stole Miss Muffet's special bowl? How do you know?

Missing Words:
1.pig 2.pig 3.tarts 4.window 5.fat 6.lean
The Jack of Hearts stole the special Sunday cereal bowl. He was the only one who knew the color of the bowl.

MOTHER GOOSE NAME SEARCH

How many Mother Goose characters can you find?

Y	S	G	O	Z	U	M	I	S	S	J	A	E	P	W
T	M	T	X	L	M	Y	D	X	A	B	O	V	E	L
P	T	T	R	H	D	K	S	C	S	T	D	E	E	U
M	A	E	O	A	X	K	J	F	R	W	Q	P	C	
U	H	G	F	B	E	S	I	A	L	I	E	U	O	Y
D	C	U	C	F	P	H	H	N	L	T	G	L	B	L
Y	W	S	I	R	U	S	F	L	G	M	O	A	S	O
T	W	K	A	U	Y	M	I	O	X	C	J	M	I	C
P	K	T	K	B	Y	E	B	V	N	E	O	J	J	K
M	M	V	B	R	W	V	D	D	C	E	O	L	Q	E
U	S	O	A	I	P	S	K	A	C	D	E	P	E	T
H	B	M	N	I	B	O	R	K	C	O	C	U	D	T
J	O	K	S	X	O	L	U	T	A	I	R	S	Q	O
M	I	E	U	L	B	Y	O	B	E	L	T	T	I	L
E	J	A	C	K	A	N	D	J	I	L	L	D	U	L

Names to Find

Cock Robin	Bobby Shaftoe	Bo Peep	Wee Willie Winkie
Humpty Dumpty	Jack and Jill	Jack Sprat	
Little Boy Blue	Lucy Locket	Mary	
Old King Cole	Queen of Hearts	Tom	

MOTHER GOOSE EDITIONS

Brian Wildsmith's Mother Goose: A Collection of Nursery Rhymes. Danbury, CT, Franklin Watts, 1965.

Here Comes Mother Goose. Comp. by Iona Opie. Illus. by Rosemary Wells. Cambridge, MA, Candlewick Press, 1999.

I Saw Esau. Comp. Iona and Peter Opie. Illus. by Maurice Sendak. Cambridge, MA, Candlewick Press, 1992.

Marguerite de Angeli's Book of Nursery Rhymes and Mother Goose. New York, Doubleday, 1979.

Mary Had A Little Lamb by Sarah Hale. Illus. by Sally Mavor. New York, Orchard, 1995.

Mother Goose in Spanish. Trans. Alistair Reed. Illus. by Barbara Cooney. New York, Crowell, 1968.

Mother Goose Nursery Rhymes. Illus. by Arthur Rackham. Danbury, CT, Franklin Watts, 1969.

Mother Goose or the Old Nursery Rhymes. Illus. by Kate Greenaway. New York, Frederik Warne, 1882.

Mother Goose Picture Riddles: A Book of Rebuses. Illus. by Lisl Weil. New York, Holiday House, 1981.

Movable Mother Goose by Robert Sabuda. New York, Simon & Schuster, 1999.

My Very First Mother Goose. Comp. Iona Opie. Illus. by Rosemary Wells. Cambridge, MA, Candlewick Press, 1996.

Nursery Rhyme Book. Ed. Andrew Lang. Illus. by L. Leslie Brooke. New York, Frederik Warne, 1947.

Oxford Dictionary of Nursery Rhymes. Comp. by Iona and Peter Opie. New York, Oxford, 1951.

The Real Mother Goose. Illus. by Blanche Fisher Wright. Chicago, Rand McNally, 1965.

AESOP'S FABLES

Solve the cryptograms. Find titles of seven Aesop's Fables.

The code:

A B C D E F G H I J K L M N O P Q R S T U V W X Y Z
Y Z X W A I R K M V P H Q J S C G U N T E L F B O D

1. Y   F S H I   M J   N K A A C N   X H S T K M J R

    __ _____ ____ _____ _____

2. K Y U A   Y J W   T K A   T S U T S M N A

    _____ _____ _____ _____

3. R S S N A   F M T K   T K A   R S H W A J   A R R N

    _____ _____ _____ _____ _____

4. R U Y N N K S C C A U   Y J W   T K A   Y J T N

    _____ _____ _____ _____

5. Z A H H M J R   T K A   X Y T

    _____ _____ ____

6. W S R   M J   T K A   Q Y J R A U

    _____ ____ _____ _____

7. H M S J   Y J W   T K A   Q S E N A

    _____ _____ _____ _____

Key: 1. A Wolf in Sheep's Clothing 2. Hare and the Tortoise 3. Goose with the Golden Eggs 4. Grasshopper and the Ants 5. Belling the Cat 6. Dog in the Manger 7. Lion and the Mouse

AESOP'S FABLES WORD SEARCH

Use the clues at the bottom of the page to search for the last word in each title.

g	s	s	m	n	p	s	m
n	h	e	e	o	n	i	a
i	a	p	r	g	u	t	n
h	d	a	m	c	g	s	g
t	o	r	t	o	i	s	e
o	w	g	t	a	u	s	r
l	h	w	h	n	c	s	s
c	o	g	o	m	h	e	e

1. Dog in the _____

2. Wolf in Sheep's _____

3. Lion and the _____

4. Belling the _____

5. Dog and His _____

6. Hare and the _____

7. Wind and the _____

8. Fox and the _____

Key: 1. manger 2. clothing 3. mouse 4. cat 5. shadow 6. tortoise 7. sun 8. grapes

From *Books Every Child Should Know: The Literature Quiz Book* by Nancy Polette. Westport, CT: Libraries Unlimited. Copyright © 2006.

AESOP'S FABLES

Be a Spelling Whiz!

USE ONLY THESE LETTERS: G I N C H T L O

Here are events from eight fables of Aesop. Choose from the letters above to make the missing words.

1. The warm sun ___ ___ ___ up the day.

2. Take away one letter and add one letter to make the missing word.

   The greedy dog wanted a ___ ___ ___ of meat.

3. Choose different four letters to make the missing word.

   The bell on the cat went under its ___ ___ ___ ___.

4. Take away two letters and add two letters to make the missing word.

   A small mouse helped a big ___ ___ ___ ___.

5. Take away two letters and add two letters to make the missing word.

   A grasshopper with no food will become ___ ___ ___ ___.

6. Add one letter to make the missing word.

   Being slow and steady is a good ___ ___ ___ ___ ___.

7. Move the letters in #6 around to make the missing word.

   The sun cannot shine at ___ ___ ___ ___ ___.

8. Use all of the letters to make the missing word.

   The sun made the man take off his ___ ___ ___ ___ ___ ___ ___ ___.

Key: 1. lit 2. lot 3. chin 4. lion 5. thin 6. thing 7. night 8. clothing

AESOP'S FABLES MATCHING GAME

Match the title of each fable with the lesson it teaches.

1. _____ The Wind and the Sun

2. _____ A Wolf in Sheep's Clothing

3. _____ Hare and the Tortoise

4. _____ Goose with the Golden Eggs

5. _____ Grasshopper and the Ants

6. _____ Belling the Cat

7. _____ Dog and His Shadow

8. _____ Lion and the Mouse

A. Little friends might prove to be great friends.

B. Gentleness can accomplish what force cannot.

C. Slow and steady wins the race.

D. It does not pay to pretend to be what you are not.

E. Greediness can cause one to lose everything.

F. It takes time to win success.

G. He who plays all the time will have to suffer for it.

H. It is easier to suggest a plan than to carry it out.

Key: 1. B 2. D 3. C 4. F 5. G 6. H, 7. E 8. A

From *Books Every Child Should Know: The Literature Quiz Book*
by Nancy Polette. Westport, CT: Libraries Unlimited. Copyright © 2006.

AESOP'S FABLES

Play "The Answer Is ..."

Example:

1. The answer is "They are too green and sour." What is the question? (From *The Fox and the Grapes*)

   What did the fox say about the grapes when he could not reach them?

2. The answer is "It was another dog with a large piece of meat." What is the question? (From *The Dog and the Shadow*)

   _____

3. The answer is "The crow was able to quench his thirst." What is the question? (From *The Crow and the Pitcher*)

   _____

4. The answer is "What beautiful wings you have and what bright eyes." What is the question? (From *The Fox and the Crow*)

   _____

5. The answer is "Since you could sing all summer, you may dance all winter." What is the question? (From *The Grasshopper and the Ants*)

   _____

6. The answer is "The mouse set to work to nibble the knot in the cord." What is the question? (From *The Lion and the Mouse*)

   _____

7. The answer is "The hare treated the race as a joke and decided to take a nap." What is the question? (From *The Hare and the Tortoise*)

   _____

8. The answer is "He threw his cape to the ground." What is the question? (From *The Wind and the Sun*)

   _____

Key: Sample questions (Answers may vary) 2. What did the dog see in the water? 3. When the crow raised the water level in the pitcher with pebbles, what happened? 4. What did the fox say to the crow? 5. What did the ants say to the grasshopper? 6. How did the mouse free sun cause the man to do?the lion from the net? 7. Why did the hare lose the race with the tortoise?, 8. What did the sun cause the man to do?

FABLES

Aesop's Fables by Barbara Bader. Illus. by Arthur Geisert. Boston, Houghton-Mifflin, 1991.

Aesop's Fables trans. by V. Vernon Jones. Illus. by Arthur Rackham. Danbury, CT, Franklin Watts, 1968.

Aesop's Fables by Jerry Pinkney. New York, North-South, 2000.

Aesop's Fables by Fulvio Testa. New York, Barron's, 1989.

Aesop's Fables by Lisbeth Zwerger. Boston, Picture Book Studios, 1989.

The Ant and the Grasshopper retold by Amy Poole. New York, Holiday House, 2000.

The Caldecott Aesop by Randolph Caldecott. New York, Doubleday, 1978.

The Lion and the Mouse by Ed Young. New York, Doubleday, 1980.

The Lion and the Mouse and Other Aesop's Fables by Doris Orgel. Illus. by Bert Kitchen. New York, Dorling Kindersley, 2001.

Once A Mouse by Marcia Brown. New York, Scribner's, 1961.

A Sip of Aesop by Jane Yolen. Illus. by Karen Barbour. New York, Blue Sky, 1995.

Seven Blind Mice by Ed Young. New York, Philomel, 1992.

Town Mouse, Country Mouse by Jan Brett. New York, Putnam, 1994.

Fables of Jean de la Fontaine

Fables of La Fontaine. Trans. by Marianne Moore. New York, Viking, 1954.

The Rich Man and the Shoemaker. Illus. by Brian Wildsmith. Danbury, CT, Franklin Watts, 1965.

The Turtle and the Two Ducks: Animal Fables from La Fontaine. Retold by Patricia Plante and David Bergman. Illus. by Anne Rockwell. New York, Crowell, 1981.

GREEK MYTHS

Solve the cryptograms. Find the titles of nine Greek myths.

The code:

A	B	C	D	E	F	G	H	I	J	K	L	M	N	O	P	Q	R	S	T	U	V	W	X	Y	Z
C	K	J	F	I	A	Q	X	W	M	O	G	R	N	D	P	Z	Y	E	H	L	B	T	V	S	U

1. X I Y J L G I E   C N F   P Y D R H X I L E

     _____   _____   _____

2. F I R I H I Y

     _____

3. J L P W F   C N F   P E S J X I

     _____   _____   _____

4. D Y P X I L E

     _____

5. W J C Y L E   C N F   F C I F C G L E

     _____   _____   _____

6. P X C I H X D N

     _____

7. K I G G I Y D P   X D N

     _____   _____

8. C H C G C N H E   Y C J I

     _____   _____

9. H X I   Q D G F I N   H D L J X

     _____   _____   _____

Key: 1. Hercules and Prometheus 2. Demeter 3. Cupid and Psyche
4. Orpheus 5. Icarus and Daedalus 6. Phaethon 7. Bellerophon
8. Atalanta's Race 9. The Golden Touch

GREEK AND ROMAN MYTHS: HOMOPHONES

Homophones are words that sound the same but have different meanings and different spellings.

Example: Does one *right* a word or *write* a word?

Circle the 25 misused homophones in this *Story of Persephone.* Above each circled word, write the correct homophone.

The ancient Greeks believed that Persephone is the cymbal of spring. She was the daughter of Demeter, the goddess of the harvest. This is how the berth of spring came to bee. In the coarse of gathering flowers one day, Persephone was captured by Pluto, god of the Underworld. He fell in love with her after being shot by one of Cupid's arrows. Despite her whales, he took her strait to his kingdom and trust her up her there. Her wrists were soar from the ropes. Daily she preyed for the pane to lessen. Demeter searched for her and and mast an attack which caused the earth to be bear until she could fined her daughter.

Zeus, who rained over all the gods, finally intervened and sent Hermes to the underworld to locate Persephone, who sat pail and joyless by the side of the callus Pluto. It was a terrible seen. Hermes's message was that she wood be returned to her mother if she could be shone not to have tasted food wile in the realm of the dead. Persephone had eaten four cedes of a pomegranate, and so was destined to spend one-third of the year at the seat of Pluto's thrown. During that time, nature dyes. When Persephone returns in the spring, she sees the first flour, followed by week after weak of summer and the harvest of autumn.

Key: 1. symbol 2. birth 3. be 4. course 5. wails 6. straight 7. trussed 8. sore 9. prayed 10. pain 11. massed 12. bare 13. find 14. reigned 15. pale 16. callous 17. scene 18. would 19. shown 20. while 21. seeds 22. throne 23. dies 24. flower 25. week

From *Books Every Child Should Know: The Literature Quiz Book* by Nancy Polette. Westport, CT: Libraries Unlimited. Copyright © 2006.

GREEK AND ROMAN MYTHS: MATCHING GAME

How sharp is your god and monster memory? Match each with its description.

Greek and Roman Gods and Goddesses

1. Zeus _____

2. Mars _____

3. Minerva _____

4. Jupiter _____

5. Neptune _____

6. Demeter _____

a. Roman goddess of wisdom

b. Greek goddess of agriculture

c. Ruler of the Greek gods

d. Roman god of the sea

e. Roman god of war

f. Ruler of the Roman gods

Monsters of Mythology

1. Medusa _____

2. Minotaur _____

3. Cyclops _____

4. Lernean Hydra _____

5. Cerberus _____

6. Geryon _____

7. Stymphalian Birds _____

8. Chimera _____

a. Serpent with nine heads, one of which is immortal

b. Giant with one eye

c. Man-eaters with bronze feet and sharp features

d. Woman with hair of snakes and hideous face

e. Half human, half bull

f. Three-headed dog with serpent's tail

g. Three bodies joined at the waist, thus having six hands and feet, and three heads

h. Fire-breathing monster

> Key: Gods & Goddesses: 1. c 2. e 3. a 4. f 5. d 6. b
> Monsters: 1. d 2. e 3. b 4. a 5. f 6. g 7. c 8. h

GREEK AND ROMAN MYTHS: SCAVENGER HUNT

According to mythology, Heracles, a fierce warrior, was the mightiest mortal ever to live. Because he was only half-divine, he had to earn his immortality on Mount Olympus, the mountain of the gods. He was forced to perform twelve impossible labors for King Eurytheus in order to become immortal.

Help Heracles on his journey. Search the library shelves. Write the topic for each Dewey number on the line following the number.

1. Slay the Nemean **599.75**_____, a beast no **355.82**_____ can kill.

2. Slay the Lernean **593.71**_____, a creature with nine heads, one of which is immortal.

3. Bring back alive the Arcadian Stag with antlers of **553.4**_____ and hooves of silver.

4. Destroy the Erymanthian Boar that lives high on a **551.4**_____.

5. Clean the Augean **636.1**_____'s stables in one day.

6. Drive away and destroy the man-eating Stymphalian **598.2**_____.

7. Take captive the savage **636.2**_____of Crete.

8. Catch the man-eating **636.1**_____ of Diomedes, **909**_____ of Thrace.

9. Bring back the girdle of Hippolyta, **909.82**_____ of the Amazons.

10. Capture the oxen of the **001.94**_____ Geryon.

11. Bring back the Golden **634.1**_____of the Hesperides

12. Bring from **292.21**_____ the three-headed **636.7**_____ Cerberus.

Key: 1. lion, weapons 2. Hydra (monster) 3. gold 4. mountain
5. horses 6. birds 7. bull 8. horses, king 9. queen 10. monster
11. apples 12. Hades, dog

GREEK AND ROMAN MYTHS

Cupid and Psyche by Charlotte M. Craft. Illus. by Kinuko Craft. New York, Morrow, 1996.

D'Aulaire's Book of Greek Myths by Ingri and Edgar Parin d'Aulaire. New York, Doubleday, 1962.

Greek Gods and Heroes. Retold by Robert Graves. New York, Laurel Leaf, 1995.

Hercules. Retold by Bernard Evslin. Illus. by Joseph A. Smith. New York, Morrow, 1984.

Heroes and Monsters of Greek Myths. Retold by Bernard Evslin. Illus. by Willia Hunter. New York, Scholastic, 1970.

Jason and the Argonauts. Retold by Bernard Evslin. Illus. by Bert Dodson. New York, Morrow, 1986.

Jason and the Golden Fleece. Retold and illus. by Leonard Everett Fisher. New York, Holiday House, 1990.

King Midas: The Golden Touch. Illus. by Demi. New York, McElderry, 2002.

The Olympians. Retold and illus. by Leonard Everett Fisher. New York, Holiday House, 1984.

Pandora by Robert Burleigh. Illus. by Ray Colon. San Diego, Harcourt, 2002.

Pegasus, the Flying Horse. Retold by Jane Yolen. Illus. by Li Ming. New York, Dutton, 1998.

Persephone. Illus. by Warwick Hutton. New York, McElderry, 1994.

Roman Myths. Retold by Geraldine McCaughrean. Illus. by Emma Clark. New York, McElderry, 2001.

Theseus and the Minotaur. Illus. by Leonard Everett Fisher. New York, Holiday House, 1990.

The Trojan War and the Adventures of Odysseus by Padric Colum. Illus. by Barry Moser. New York, Morrow, 1997.

FOLKTALES AND FAIRYTALES FROM GERMANY

Solve the cryptograms to find the titles of some favorite tales.

The code:

A B C D E F G H I J K L M N O P Q R S T U V W X Y Z
P Z H D R G I N S K L J A O V C F X Q W M T B U E Y

1. W N R   R J T R Q   P O D   W N R   Q N V R A P L R X

    _____   _____   _____   _____   _____

2. W N R   Z X R A R O   W V B O   A M Q S H S P O Q

    _____   _____   _____   _____

3. N P O Q R J   P O D   I X R W R J

    _____   _____   _____

4. W N R   G S Q N R X A P O   P O D   N S Q B S G R

    _____   _____   _____   _____

5. X P C M O Y R J

    _____

6. Q O V B   B N S W R

    _____   _____

7. X M A C J R Q W S J W Q L S O

    _____

8. Q J R R C S O I   Z R P M W E

    _____   _____

Key: 1. The Elves and the Shoemaker 2. The Bremen Town Musicians 3. Hansel and Gretel 4. The Fisherman and His Wife 5. Rapunzel 6. Snow White 7. Rumplestiltskin 8. Sleeping Beauty

From *Books Every Child Should Know: The Literature Quiz Book* by Nancy Polette. Westport, CT: Libraries Unlimited. Copyright © 2006.

FOLKTALES AND FAIRYTALES FROM GERMANY: SECRET WORD

Circle the letter under True if the statement is true.

Circle the letter under False if the statement is false.

Place the circled letters in order on the lines at the bottom of the page to reveal the name of one of the brothers who collected the tales.

	TRUE	FALSE
1. The Elves helped a baker make bread.	D	J
2. There were four Bremen Town Musicians.	A	E
3. Hansel and Gretel used pebbles to find their way home.	C	M
4. Ashputtel is the German Sleeping Beauty.	W	O
5. The Fisherman and His Wife got presents from a shark.	A	B
6. Rapunzel's father picked rampion in the witch's garden.	G	N
7. Snow White was helped by eight dwarves.	E	R
8. A poor girl gave Rumplestiltskin her necklace.	I	U
9. Sleeping Beauty pricked herself with a spindle.	M	C
10. The Peasant's Clever Daughter found gold in the field.	M	F

— — — — —   — — — — —

Secret Name: Jacob Grimm

FOLKTALES AND FAIRYTALES FROM GERMANY: WORD SEARCH

Find these characters from German folk and fairy tales in the word search: Ashputtel, Elves, Snow White, Dwarves, Gretel, Hansel, Dog, Cat, Witch, Donkey, Rooster.

A	E	L	V	E	S	M	Y
S	T	W	D	O	G	W	E
H	I	L	L	L	S	X	K
P	H	A	N	S	E	L	N
U	W	C	W	D	V	E	O
T	W	A	I	C	R	T	D
T	O	T	T	M	A	E	L
E	N	K	C	O	W	R	G
L	S	F	H	G	D	G	E
R	O	O	S	T	E	R	M

From *Books Every Child Should Know: The Literature Quiz Book*
by Nancy Polette. Westport, CT: Libraries Unlimited. Copyright © 2006.

FOLKTALES AND FAIRYTALES FROM GERMANY: CHOOSE THE RIGHT WORD

1. The word that best describes *Snow White* lost in the forest is:

    A) embarrassed   B) triumphant   C) afflicted   D) vulnerable

    because_____

2. The word that best describes the witch in *Hansel and Gretel* is

    A) mystical, B) magnificent, C) malevolent, D) sympathetic

    because_____

3. The word that best describes *Rapunzel* in the tower is:

    A) forsaken, B) ambitious, C) jubilant, D) mellow

    because_____

4. The word that best describes the *Bremen Town Musicians* is:

    A) free, B) lonely, C) insecure, D) nauseated

    because_____

5. The word that best describes the 13th wise woman in *Sleeping Beauty* is:

    A) ambitious, B) putrid, C) awesome, D) revengeful

    because_____

6. The word that best describes the stepmother's feeling for *Snow White* is:

    A) jealousy, B) admiration, C) kinship, D) curiosity

    because_____

7. Which word best describes *Rumplestiltskin* when the queen spoke his name?

    A) taciturn, B) terrified, C) frustrated, D) constrained

    because_____

Key: 1. D 2. C 3. A 4. A 5. D, 6. A 7. C

FOLKTALES AND FAIRYTALES FROM GERMANY

Bremen Town Musicians retold and illus. by Ilse Plume. New York, Doubleday, 1980.

Elves and the Shoemaker. Illus. by Bernadette Watts. New York, North-South, 1986.

Fisherman and His Wife. Retold by John Warren Stewig. Illus. by Margot Tomes. New York, Holiday House, 1988.

Frog Prince. Trans. by Naomi Lewis. Illus. by Binette Schroeder. New York, North-South, 1998.

Hansel and Gretel. Illus. by Paul Galdone. Austin, TX, McGraw-Hill, 1982.

Iron John. Illus. by Trina Schart Hyman. New York, Holiday House, 1994.

The Juniper Tree and Other Tales from Grimm. Trans. by Lore Segal. Illus. by Maurice Sendak. New York, Farrar, Straus & Giroux, 1973.

Little Red Cap. Trans. Elizabeth Crawford. Illus. by Lisbeth Zwerger. New York, Morrow, 1983.

Little Red Riding Hood. Illus. by Trina Schart Hyman. New York, Holiday House, 1983.

Ouch! by Natalie Babbit. Illus. by Fred Marcellino. New York, HarperCollins, 1998.

Princess Furball. Retold by Charlotte Huck. Illus. by Anita Lobel. New York, Greenwillow, 1989.

Rapunzel. Retold by Aliz Berenzy. New York, Holt, 1995.

Rumplestiltskin. Illus. by Paul Galdone. Boston, Houghton-Mifflin, 1985.

The Seven Ravens. Trans. Elizabeth Crawford. Illus. by Lisbeth Zwerger. New York, Morrow, 1981.

Sleeping Beauty. Retold and illus. by Trina Schart Hyman. Boston, Little Brown, 1974.

Snow White and the Seven Dwarfs. Trans. by Paul Heins. Illus. by Trina chart Hyman. Boston, Little Brown, 1974.

The Table, the Donkey and the Stick. Illus. by Paul Galdone. McGraw-Hill, 1976.

FOLKTALES AND FAIRYTALES FROM FRANCE

Solve the cryptograms and find the titles of six favorite French tales.

The Code:

A	B	C	D	E	F	G	H	I	J	K	L	M	N	O	P	Q	R	S	T	U	V	W	X	Y	Z
Y	S	V	R	W	P	I	O	H	G	J	T	Z	Q	N	X	B	U	M	C	F	E	A	L	K	D

1. T H C C T W   U W R   U H R H Q I   O N N R

    _____ _____ _____ _____

2. V H Q R W U W T T Y

    _____

3. S W Y F C K   Y Q R   C O W   S W Y M C

    _____ ____ ____ _____

4. C N Y R M   Y Q R   R H Y Z N Q R M

    _____ ____ _____

5. C O W   A O H C W   V Y C

    _____ _____ ____

6. C O W   Z Y M C W U   V Y C

    _____ _____ ____

Key: 1. Little Red Riding Hood 2. Cinderella 3. Beauty and the Beast
4. Toads and Diamonds 5. The White Cat 6. The Master Cat

FOLKTALES AND FAIRYTALES FROM FRANCE: SECRET WORD

Circle the letter under True if the statement is true.

Circle the letter under False if the statement is false.

Place the circled letters in order on the lines at the bottom of the page to find the name of the man who collected the tales.

	TRUE	FALSE
1. *Red Riding Hood* had a cake in her basket.	J	C
2. *Red Riding Hood* met a fox in the woods.	L	H
3. *Cinderella's* sisters were sour and jealous.	A	W
4. *Cinderella* lost one of her ruby slippers.	Y	R
5. *Beauty's* father lost all his money.	L	B
6. *Beauty* was forced to visit the beast.	O	E
7. The *Beast* had an aviary full of rare birds.	S	F
8. In *Toads and Diamonds* a poor girl got a gift of jewels.	P	S
9. The poor girl's sister got a gift of toads.	E	D
10. In *The White Cat*, the king asked for a dog.	R	S
11. The youngest prince meets *The White Cat*.	R	B
12. A father left his youngest son in *The Master Cat*.	A	Y
13. *The Master Cat* asked for a bag and a fancy hat.	K	U
14. *The Master Cat* caught a rabbit for the king.	L	F
15. An ogre frightened *The Master Cat*.	T	S

—— —— —— —— —— —— ——   —— —— —— —— —— —— —— ——

Secret Name: Charles Perrault

From *Books Every Child Should Know: The Literature Quiz Book* by Nancy Polette. Westport, CT: Libraries Unlimited. Copyright © 2006.

FOLKTALES AND FAIRYTALES FROM FRANCE:
TEST YOUR KNOWLEDGE

1. *Red Riding Hood* lived in

    A) the woods   B) a village   C) a cave

2. In the woods *Red Riding Hood* met

    A) a wolf   B) a fox   C) a lion

3. *Cinderella* had

    A) ruby slippers   B) glass slippers   C) golden slippers

4. In *Beauty and the Beast*, Beauty asked her father to bring her

    A) diamonds   B) a rose   C) a new gown

5. In *Beauty and the Beast*, Beauty had

    A) three sisters   B) no sisters   C) two sisters

6. In *Beauty and the Beast*, Beauty liked to

    A) hear birds sing   B) play the harp   C) wear pretty dresses

7. In *Toads and Diamonds* the youngest daughter helped

    A) an old man   B) an old woman   C) an injured deer

8. In *Toads and Diamonds*, the older sister refused to help

    A) an old man   B) an old woman   C) an injured deer

9. In *The White Cat*, twelve monkeys and twelve cats

    A) howl   B) run away   C) dance

10. In *The Master Cat*, the cat helps

    A) an old woman   B) the youngest son   C) an ogre

Key: 1. B 2. A 3. B 4. B 5. C 6. A 7. B 8. B 9. C 10. B

FOLKTALES AND FAIRYTALES FROM FRANCE: MISSING LETTERS

Fill in the missing letters. The name of the collector of these tales appears in the box. Write the name on the lines below.

1. A French tale: __ __ __ __ I N B O O T S
2. Kissed the beast: __ __ __ __ __ __ __
3. L I T T L E   __ __ __ R I D I N G H O O D
4. __ __ __ __ __ CAT
5. T H E W H I T E __ __ __
6.   __ __ __ __ __ __ slept 100 years.
7. Red Riding Hood was __ __ __ __ __ __ , not big.
8. T H E __ __ __ __ C A T

The collector of these French fairy tales is

C H A R L E S __ __ __ __ __ __ __ __

Mystery Titles: Can you guess the titles of these well-known tales?

1. The Domineering Feline.

   _____

2. One Of Fair Countenance Associated With A Formidable Creature.

   _____

3. One of Fair Countenance In The Natural Suspension Of Consciousness.

   _____

4. A Feline In Fitted Coverings For Lower Appendages.

   _____

Key: 1. Puss 2. Beauty 3. Red 4. Master 5. Cat 6. Beauty 7. Little 8. White
Mystery Titles: 1. The Master Cat 2. Beauty and the Beast 3. Sleeping Beauty 4. Puss in Boots.

From *Books Every Child Should Know: The Literature Quiz Book* by Nancy Polette. Westport, CT: Libraries Unlimited. Copyright © 2006.

A CINDERELLA MATCHING GAME

Match the Cinderella figure with her helper or her enemy.

1. _____	Tattercoats's companion	A.	ogre
2. _____	Gave Vasilissa comfort	B.	three magical animals
3. _____	Yeh Shen's friend	C.	gooseherd
4. _____	Helped Ashputtel	D.	governess
5. _____	Who Furball was to marry	E.	falcon
6. _____	Helped Pear Blossom	F.	doll
7. _____	Tricks Cenerentola	G.	fish
8. _____	Helps Tam	H.	bird
9. _____	Helps Candace	I.	foster mother
10. _____	Helps Rhodopes	J.	gris gris woman
11. _____	Helps Oona	K.	fish

Key: 1. C, 2. F, 3. G or K, 4. H, 5. A, 6. B, 7. D, 8. G, or K, 9. J, 10. E, 11. I

CINDERELLA BY MANY NAMES

Solve the cryptogram and discover the many names of Cinderella.

A	B	C	D	E	F	G	H	I	J	K	L	M
13	8	4	11	25	20	9	16	5	14	18	23	15

N	O	P	Q	R	S	T	U	V	W	X	Y	Z
24	12	22	3	21	7	6	10	19	17	2	26	1

1. __ __ __ __ __ __ __ __ __ __
   4 5 24 11 25 21 25 23 23 13

2. __ __ __ __ __ __ __ __ __
   13 7 16 22 10 6 6 25 23

3. __ __ __ __ __ __ __ __ __ __ __
   6 13 6 6 25 21 4 12 13 6 7

4. __ __ __   __ __ __ __
   26 25 16   7 16 25 24

5. __ __ __ __ __ __ __ __
   21 16 12 11 12 22 25 7

6. __ __ __ __   __ __ __ __ __ __ __
   22 25 13 21   8 23 12 7 7 12 15

7. __ __ __ __ __ __ __ __
   19 13 7 5 23 5 7 13

8. __ __ __ __   __ __ __ __
   15 12 7 7   9 12 17 24

> Key: 1. Cinderella 2. Ashputtel 3. Tattercoats 4. Yeh Shen
> 5. Rhodopes 6. Pear Blossom 7. Vasilisa 8. Moss Gown

A CINDERELLA SCAVENGER HUNT

Go to the library shelves. Find the topic for each Dewey number in the story. Write each topic in the blanks to help Cinderella get to the ball.

The stepmother and stepsisters went to the ball dressed in their finest. Cinderella waited and waited for her fairy godmother to arrive but she did not come.

I really want to go to the ball at the **(1) 725.17** _____. There will be **(2) 781** _____ and **(3) 792** _____ and wonderful **(4) 641** _____. I might even meet a prince who will take me away from my life of hard work. I will find other ways to get to the ball, Cinderella declared. Yeh Shen had a magic **(5) 597** _____ to help her. I will head for the nearest **(6) 551.4** _____ to see if I can find one. On second thought, the ball would be over before I got back. I must think of another idea.

"Some Cinderellas have been helped by **(7) 598** _____. I will go outside and stand under a **(8) 582** _____ and perhaps one will come to me. If the forest is near a road maybe a **(9) 636.1** _____ will wander by and I can ride to the ball, that way. Even if I do find a way to get to the ball, I have no beautiful **(10) 646.3** _____."

Just then the **(11) 551.5** _____ changed. The sky turned as bright as day. Cinderella heard a sound and turned to see a magic **(12) 636.8** _____. It twitched its tail three times and Cinderella was dressed in a beautiful gown and adorned with magnificent **(13) 739.2** _____. Another twitch of the tail and she was sent to the ball by **(14) 793.8** _____.

Since she did not have to watch the **(15) 529** _____, Cinderella and the prince fell in love, and they were married that very evening. She never saw her stepmother or stepsisters again.

Key: 1. castle 2. music 3. dancing 4. food 5. fish 6. ocean 7. birds 8. tree 9. horse 10. clothing 11. weather 12. cat 13. jewelry 14. magic 15. time

TALES FROM FRANCE

Beauty and the Beast by Mme. de Beaumont. Illus. by Jan Brett. Boston, Houghton-Mifflin, 1989.

The Magic Porridge Pot. Illus. by Paul Galdone. Boston, Clarion, 1979.

Puss In Boots. Illus. by Paul Galdone. Boston, Clarion, 1976.

Stone Soup. Illus. by Marcia Brown. New York, Scribner's, 1947.

Three Perfect Peaches by Cynthia deFelice. Illus. by Irene Trias. New York, Orchard, 1995.

Three Sacks of Truth by Eric Kimmell. Illus. by Robert Rayevskt. New York, Holiday House, 1993.

Toads and Diamonds by Charlotte Huck. Illus. by Anita Lobel. New York, Greenwillow, 96.

Twelve Dancing Princesses by Marianna Mayer. Illus. by Kinuko Craft. New York, Morrow, 1994.

The White Cat by Robert San Souci. Illus. by Gennady Spirin. New York, Orchard, 1990.

Cinderella Variants

Ashputtel: A Cinderella Tale From Germany, translated from the Grimm Tales by Ralph Manheim. New York, Doubleday, 1977.

The Brocaded Slipper by Lynette Dyer Vuong. Illus. by Vo-Ding Mai. Old Tappan, NJ, Addison-Wesley, 1982.

Cenerentola found in *Favorite Fairy Tales Told In Italy* by Virginia Haviland. Illus. by Evaline Ness. Boston, Little-Brown, 1965.

Cinder Edna by Ellen Jackson. Illus. by Kevin O Malley. New York, Lothrop, 1994.

Cinderella by Charles Perrault. Illus. by Marcia Brown. New York, Scribners, 1954.

The Egyptian Cinderella by Shirley Climo. Illus. by Ruth Heller. New York, HarperCollins, 1989.

The Korean Cinderella by Shirley Climo. Illus. by Ruth Heller. New York, HarperCollins, 1993.

Moss Gown by William H. Hooks. Illus. by Donald Carrick. Boston, Clarion, 1987.

Mufaro's Beautiful Daughters written and illus. by John Steptoe. New York, Scholastic, 1987.

Princess Furball by Charlotte Huck. Illus. by Anita Lobel. New York, Greenwillow Books, 1989.

The Rough-Face Girl by Rafe Martin. Illus. by David Shannon. New York, Putnam's, 1992.

HANS CHRISTIAN ANDERSEN TALES

The words of titles of Hans Christian Andersen tales have been replaced by synonyms. Write the actual titles.

1. The Unrelenting Stannic Combatant

_____

2. The Minute Female with Enabled Conflagration

_____

3. The Monarch's Unprecedented Adornment

_____

4. The Sovereign's Female Offspring and the Legume

_____

5. The Waterfowl's Unsightly Progeny

_____

6. The Miniscule Oceanid

_____

7. The Ruling Female Monarch Inundated with White Crystaline Precipitation

_____

8. The Outer Coverings of Human Appendages with Blush Pigment

_____

Key. 1. The Steadfast Tin Soldier 2. The Little Match Girl 3. The Emperor's New Clothes 4. The Princess and the Pea 5. The Ugly Duckling 6. The Little Mermaid 7. The Snow Queen 8. The Red Shoes

From *Books Every Child Should Know: The Literature Quiz Book* by Nancy Polette. Westport, CT: Libraries Unlimited. Copyright © 2006.

TALES BY HANS CHRISTIAN ANDERSEN: MATCHING GAME

Match the theme of each tale with the title.

1. _____ Vanity can cause one to be easily fooled.

2. _____ Life can be cruel but rewards are found in Heaven.

3. _____ Nature cannot be replaced with modern technology.

4. _____ It is not wise to trust strangers.

5. _____ Undying love is not always rewarded.

6. _____ Wishing for the impossible brings sadness.

7. _____ It takes time to realize one's full potential.

8. _____ Love for family combined with courage can win the day.

The Tales:

A. *The Snow Queen*

B. *The Wild Swans*

C. *The Emperor's New Clothes*

D. *The Little Match Girl*

E. *The Ugly Duckling*

F. *The Nightingale*

G. *The Steadfast Tin Soldier*

H. *The Little Mermaid*

Key: 1. C 2. D 3. F 4. A 5. G 6. H 7. E 8. B

THE FATHER OF THE MODERN FAIRY TALE

Hans Christian Andersen (1805–1875)

Underline the correct look-alike word as it should appear in this short biography of Hans Christian Andersen.

While Andersen's name is well known today his **1** (ascent/assent) to fame was slow. Born in Odense, he suffered from the **2** (adverse/averse) **3** (affects/effects) of poverty and neglect during his childhood. He often played hookey from school and spent time on the wharves. There he listened to the **4** (bazaar/bizarre) tales of the fishwives. One of his ambitions was to **5** (appraise/apprise) others of these tales.

When he was fourteen he **6** (quit/quiet) school completely and ran away from home. He got a job at the Royal Theatre in Copenhagen and a period of time **7** (elapsed/relapsed) before he began writing his stories.

Andersen's first novel, *The Improviser*, was published in 1835 and his first book of fairy tales was published that same year. Andersen traveled **8** (intensively/extensively} in Europe, Asia, and Africa. Despite his success he was often **9** (dissolute/desolate), a feeling which is found in his tale of *The Ugly Ducking* before the duckling becomes a swan. Like the duckling, Anderson suffered from the **10** (allusion/delusion) that he was unappreciated. This is one reason he earned the nickname "The Melancholy Dane."

Key: 1. ascent 2. adverse 3. effects 4. bizarre 5. apprise 6. quit 7. elasped 8. extensively 9. desolate 10. delusion

---

FOLKTALES AND FAIRYTALES FROM SCANDINAVIA

Solve the cryptograms to decode sentences from four exciting tales.

The Code:

A B C D E F G H I J K L M N O P Q R S T U V W X Y Z

O J C G M H Q A D Z W E P U V R L S Y X F B K N I T

1. From *The Three Billy Goats Gruff*

   KAV DY XSDRRDUQ VBMS PI JSDGQM?

   ___ ___ ___ ___ ___ ___ ___ ___ ___ ___

   ___ ___ ___ ___ ___ ___ ___ ___ ___ ___ ___?

2. From *The Pancake*

   EWZA SZLXZJW, EKL'M AKGG UK IZUM.

   ___ ___ ___ ___ ___ ___ ___ ___ ___ ___ ___ ___ ,___ ___ ___ ___'___

   ___ ___ ___ ___ ___ ___ ___ ___ ___ ___

3. From *The Princess on the Glass Hill*

   AV AV DX' Y IVF XAOX QVJJEMY FR VFS AOI

   ___ ___ ___ ___ ___ ___' ___ ___ ___ ___ ___ ___ ___

   ___ ___ ___ ___ ___ ___ ___ ___ ___ ___ ___ ___ ___

4. From *East o' the Sun and West o' the Moon*

   OX XAM GVVS XAM HOXAMS YOK O QSMOX KADXM JMOS

   ___ ___ ___ ___ ___ ___ ___ ___ ___ ___ ___ ___ ___

   ___ ___ ___ ___ ___ ___ ___ ___ ___ ___ ___ ___

Key:
1. Who is tripping over my bridge?
2. Dear pancake don't roll so fast.
3. Ho Ho it's you that gobbles up our hay.
4. At the door the father saw a great White Bear.

FOLKTALES AND FAIRYTALES FROM SCANDINAVIA: HEADLINES

Unscramble the titles. Place the boxed words on the lines below to create a fairy tale newspaper headline.

1. ┌─────┐ T A C
   │ T A F │
   └─────┘

2. T M S A R E ┌─────┐
             │ T A C │
             └─────┘

3. ┌────────┐ D N A   S I H   S R E H T O R B
   │ T O B O S │
   └────────┘

4. N U S   D N A   ┌────────────┐   F O   H E T   O O M N
                 │ E R T H G U A D │
                 └────────────┘

5. E L T T I L   D L O   N A M O W   ┌─────┐   H E T
                                   │ D N A │
                                   └─────┘
   Y R G N U   H   T A C

6. S M A E R T   ┌────────┐
               │ D M I A │
               └────────┘

7. ┌──────┐ ┌────┐ H E T   N U S   D N A
   │ T S A E │ │ F O │
   └──────┘ └────┘
   T W S E   F O   ┌──────┐   ┌──────┐
                 │ H E T │   │ O O N M │
                 └──────┘   └──────┘

EXTRA! *FAIRY TALE TIMES* EXTRA!

_____

_____

Key: 1. Fat Cat 2. Master Cat 3. Boots and his Brothers 4. Sun and Daughter of the Moon 5. Little Old Woman and the Hungry Cat 6. Master Maid 7. East of the Sun and West of the Moon
Headline: Fat Cat Boots Daughter And Maid East of the Moon

FOLKTALES AND FAIRYTALES FROM SCANDINAVIA

A Dewey Decimal Scavenger Hunt

The Maid on the Glass Mountain
from *East o' the Sun and West o' the Moon* by Peter Asbjornsen

Visit the library shelves and write the topic for each Dewey number on the line after the number.

It is midnight on St. John's night and Cinderlad is crouched in the hayloft of the **1) 630** _____ waiting to see what strange creature comes on this special night each year to eat all of the **2) 584.9** _____ in the meadow. The two previous years his brothers had been sent to watch but were so frightened by the clatter and the noise that they ran away. A rumble in the distance grew louder and louder. The hayloft shook and Cinderlad was thrown to the floor. Picking himself up, he marched outside to see a huge, gleaming **3) 636.1** _____ with the **4) 739.7** _____ of a **5) 940.1** _____ on the ground beside it. Cinderlad jumped on the horse and rode it to a hiding place, and then went home to his **6) 646.78** _____. For three years in a row, Cinderlad kept watch, and each year found a horse larger and grander than the last.

Now in this same country there was a **7) 909** _____ whose daughter, the princess, he would give to any man who could ride up a **8) 551.4** _____ of **9) 666.1** _____ and take three golden **10) 634.1** _____ from her lap. The **11) 940.1** _____ came from far and wide, even Cinderlad's brothers came, but no one could ride up the **12) 551.4** _____. Finally one last **13) 940.1** _____ rode up to the base of the mountain. He was on a large, grand **14) 636.1** _____ and wore a suit of copper. Who do you suppose he is? And will he win the hand of the princess? To find out read *The Maid on the Glass Mountain.*

Key: 1. farm 2. grass 3. horse 4. armor 5. knight 6. family 7. king
8. mountain 9. glass 10. apple 11. knight 12. mountain 13. knight
14. horse

From *Books Every Child Should Know: The Literature Quiz Book*
by Nancy Polette. Westport, CT: Libraries Unlimited. Copyright © 2006.

FOLKTALES AND FAIRYTALES FROM SCANDINAVIA

Boots and His Brothers by Eric Kimmel. Illus. by Kimberly Root. New York, Holiday House, 1992.

East o' the Sun and West o' the Moon by Peter Asbjornsen. New York, Dover, 1970.

Easy Work: An Old Tale by Eric Kimmel. Illus. by Andrew Glass. New York, Holiday House, 1998.

Fat Cat: A Danish Folktale by Margaret MacDonald. Illus. by Julie Pashkis. Morton Grove, IL, Whitman, 2001.

Little Old Woman and the Hungry Cat by Nancy Polette. Illus. by Frank Modell. New York, Greenwillow, 1989.

Master Maid: A Tale from Norway by Aaron Shepard. Illus. by Pauline Ellison. New York, Dial, 1997.

Race of the Birkebeiners by Lise Lunge-Larsen. Illus. by Mary Azarian. Boston, Houghton-Mifflin, 1999.

The Sun and Daughter of the Moon by Holly Huth. Illus. by Anna Voeth. New York, Atheneum, 2000.

Three Billy Goats Gruff by Peter Asbjornsen. Illus. by Marcia Brown. San Diego, Harcourt Brace, 1957.

Tales by Hans Christian Andersen

The Emperor's New Clothes. Illus. by Virginia Lee Burton. Boston, Houghton Mifflin, 1949.

Hans Christian Andersen: The Complete Fairy Tales and Stories. Trans. Erik Haugaard. New York, Doubleday, 1974.

The Little Match Girl. Illus. by Jerry Pinkney. New York, Putnam, 2002.

Little Mermaids and Ugly Ducklings: Favorite Tales. Illus. by Gennadii Spirin. San Diego, Chronicle Books, 2001.

The Nightingale. Illus. by Lisbeth Zwerger. New York, North-South, 1999.

The Snow Queen. Trans. Anthea Bell. Illus. by Bernadette Watts. Boston, Picture Book Studio, 1985.

The Steadfast Tin Soldier. Retold by Tor Seidler. Illus. by Fred Marcellino. New York, HarperCollins, 1992.

The Ugly Duckling. Illus. by Jerry Pinkney. New York, William Morrow, 1999.

The Wild Swans. Retold by Amy Ehrlich. Illus. by Susan Jeffers. New York, Dial, 1981.

FOLKTALES AND FAIRYTALES FROM THE BRITISH ISLES

Find folktale and fairy tale titles by solving the cryptograms.

Use this code:

A B C D E F G H I J K L M N O P Q R S T U V W X Y Z
G P B N W A O U D T J E L Q R S Z Y C I V K M H X F

1. BUDBJWQ EDIIEW __ __ __ __ __ __ __ __ __ __ __ __ __

2. ODQOWYPYWGN LGQ __ __ __ __ __ __ __ __ __ __ __ __ __ __

3. UWQQX SWQQX __ __ __ __ __ __ __ __ __ __

4. TGBJ GQN IUW PWGQCIGEJ

__ __ __ __ __ __ __ __ __ __ __ __ __ __ __ __ __ __ __

5. EDIIEW YWN UWQ __ __ __ __ __ __ __ __ __ __ __ __

6. IRL IDI IRI __ __ __ __ __ __ __ __ __

7. IUYWW EDIIEW SDOC __ __ __ __ __ __ __ __ __ __ __ __ __ __ __

8. IGIIWYBRGIC __ __ __ __ __ __ __ __ __ __ __

Key: 1. Chicken Little 2. Gingerbread Man 3. Henny Penny 4. Jack and the Beanstalk 5. Little Red Hen 6. Tom Tit Tot 7. Three Little Pigs 8. Tattercoats

TALES FROM THE BRITISH ISLES: SECRET WORDS

Circle the letter under True if the statement is true.

Circle the letter under False if the statement is false.

Place the circled letters in order on the lines at the bottom of the page to find the name of the man who collected the tales.

		TRUE	FALSE
1.	Chicken Little thought the sky was falling.	J	K
2.	A magic snake helped Dick Whittington.	F	O
3.	Finn McCoul was a Scottish hero.	W	S
4.	Goldilocks broke baby bear's chair.	E	V
5.	Henny Penny ran away from the fox.	P	Y
6.	Jack sold the cow for ten beans.	D	H
7.	The second little pig built a house of bricks.	P	J
8.	The old woman bought a pig with a sixpence.	A	H
9.	Molly Whuppie outwits a witch.	R	C
10.	A girl named Burd Janet saved Tamlane.	O	F
11.	Tattercoats was shunned by her father.	D	B
12.	The Gingerbread Man said, "You can't catch me."	S	L

— — — — — — — — — — — — — —

Secret Name: Joseph Jacobs

FOLKTALES AND FAIRYTALES FROM THE BRITISH ISLES: SCAVENGER HUNT

Visit the library shelves and write the topic for each Dewey number on the line after the number. Then read the tale of *Finn M'Coul and the Giant*, retold by Nancy Polette.

Some say that Finn M'Coul, a **1) 001.9** _____ of **2) 941.5** _____ and **3) 941.1** _____ actually lived. It was a day when the **4) 523.7** _____ covered the **5) 550** _____ that Finn decided to build a **6) 624.2** _____ across the **7) 942** _____. It was then that a disturbing message arrived. The **8) 001.9** _____, Cuhullin, was arriving on a huge **9) 636.1** _____ to challenge Finn to a fight. Now everyone knows that Cuhullin can rip **10) 551.57** _____ out of the sky, pick up **11) 690** _____ with one hand and use **12) 582.16** _____ as hockey sticks. Finn was worried, so he headed home to ask his wife what could be done? Finn's wife dressed Finn in baby clothes and baked cakes with a griddle in the center of each. When Cuhullin arrived she told him that Finn was busy building **13) 624.2** _____. She asked if he would like to have tea and cakes while he was waiting. The cakes with the iron center were given to Cuhullin. A different cake was given to the baby. Cuhullin opened his mouth wide and took a big bite. CRACK! He broke a **14) 617.6** _____. Then he saw the baby munching away on a similar cake. "How amazing," he said. The child has great strength. The father's strength must be even greater. Cuhullin took off like a **15) 629.4** _____ and was never heard from again!

Key: 1. giant 2. Ireland 3. Scotland 4. sun 5. Earth 6. bridge 7. British Isles 8. giant 9. horse 10. clouds 11. houses 12. trees 13. bridges 14. tooth 15. rocket

FOLKTALES AND FAIRYTALES FROM THE BRITISH ISLES

Chicken Little. Retold and Illus. by Steven Kellogg. New York, Morrow, 1988.

Dick Whittington and His Cat. Illus. by Marcia Brown. New York, Scribner's, 1950.

Finn McCoul and His Fearless Wife by Robert Byrd. New York, Dutton, 1999.

The Gingerbread Man retold by Jim Aylesworth. Illus. by Barbara McClintock. New York, Scholastic, 1998.

Goldilocks and the Three Bears. Illus. by James Marshall. New York, Dial, 1988.

Henny Penny. Found in English Fairy Tales collected by Joseph Jacobs, 1890.

Jack and the Beanstalk. Retold and illustrated by Steven Kellogg. New York, Morrow, 1991.

Little Red Hen. Illus. by Paul Galdone. Boston, Clarion, 1999.

Master of All Masters. Found in English Fairy Tales collected by Joseph Jacobs, 1890.

Mollie Whuppie. Retold by Walter de la Mare. Illus. by Eerol LeCain. New York, Farrar, 1983.

The Old Woman and Her Pig. Retold by Eric Kimmel. New York, Holiday House, 1993.

Tam Linn by Susan Cooper. Illus. by Warwick Hutton, New York, McElderry, 1991.

Tattercoats. Retold by Flora Annie Steele. Illus. by Diane Goode. New York, Bradbury, 1976.

Tom Tit Tot. Illus. by Evaline Ness. New York, Scribner's, 1965.

Three Little Pigs. Illus. by James Marshall. New York, Dial, 1989.

The Three Sillies. Illus. by Margot Zemach. New York, Holt, 1963.

Whuppity Stoorie. Retold by Carolyn White. Illus. by S. D. Schindler. New York, Putnam, 1997.

TALES FROM ASIA AND INDIA: CHOOSE THE WORD

"Ah Cha The Sleeper," found in *Shen of the Sea* by Arthur Chrisman, Dutton, 1925.

Choose the word that best fits the feeling or situation.

1. Ah Cha was an orphan who owned seven farms, seven mills, and seven thousand pieces of gold. He was quite

   A) cautious   B) combative   C) affluent   D) vindictive

2. Year after year Ah Cha's fields produced bountiful crops. The soil was very

   A) fertile   B) hostile   C) putrid   D) pathetic

3. Ah Cha worked from early in the morning until midnight. He was

   A) obnoxious   B) industrious   C) agitated   D) tolerant

4. When Ah Cha threw a sack at a lazy cat, the cat changed into a witch. This was an amazing

   A) effigy   B) transformation   C) panorama   D) enigma

5. The angry witch cast a spell on Ah Cha, forcing him to sleep eleven hours a day. His workers stopped working and Ah Cha became

   A) arrogant   B) insensitive   C) obese   D) destitute

6. Ah Cha saved the witch who was chased by a fierce dragon that was very

   A) dynamic   B) hostile   C) altruistic   D) amiable

7. To show her gratitude the witch removed the spell and Ah Cha was

   A) demoralized   B) mournful   C) skeptical   D) elated

8. The spell that had caused him to sleep had been

   A) banished   B) exiled   C) dissipated   D) deported

Key: 1. C 2. A 3. C 4. B 5. D 6. B 7. D 8. A

TALES FROM ASIA AND INDIA: MATCHING GAME

Here are titles of tales from Asia and India with the words replaced by synonyms. Match each title with the actual title.

1. _____ A Young Male With An Annual Slumber In Triplicate
2. _____ A Young Male Engaged In Creating Representations Of Felines
3. _____ The Minute Tropical Feathered Vertebrate Displaying Courage
4. _____ The Uninhabited Cooking Vessel
5. _____ The Donation Of The Carnivorous Aquatic Reptile
6. _____ The Feline Of Unswerving Allegiance
7. _____ The Narrative Of The Short-tailed Lagomorph
8. _____ The White Metallic Amulet
9. _____ A Female Of A Luminous Celestial Body And A Male Of The Earth's Natural Satellite.
10. _____ Felines Of Warrior Aristocracy In Triplicate
11. _____ A Multitude Of Objects Doubled
12. _____ The Narrative Of Waterfowl Of Official Rank

The Tales:

A. *The Rabbit's Tale*
B. *The Empty Pot*
C. *Boy of the Three Year Nap*
D. *The Loyal Cat*
E. *The Brave Little Parrot*
F. *Three Samurai Cats*
G. *The Gift of the Crocodile*
H. *Boy Who Drew Cats*
I. *The Sun Girl and the Moon Boy*
J. *Two of Everything*
K. *Tale of the Mandarin Ducks*
L. *The Silver Charm*

Key: 1. C 2. H 3. E 4. B 5. G 6. D 7. A 8. L 9. I 10. F 11. J 12. K

TALES FROM ASIA AND INDIA

A Library Scavenger Hunt

Visit the library shelves and write the topic of each Dewey number on the line after the number.

The Korean Cinderella by Shirley Climo

In the land of **1) 951.9** _____, where creatures of **2) 763.8** _____ are as common as cabbages, lives a child named Pear Blossom. Pear Blossom is as lovely as the **3) 582.16** _____ planted in celebration of her birth, but she is mistreated by Omoni, her jealous stepmother. Omoni forces her to rise before the **4) 523.7** _____ and **5) 641.5** _____ and clean until midnight, and demands that Pear Blossom complete three tasks no human could possibly do alone. She is to fill a **6) 551.48** _____ jar with a hole in it the size of an **7) 634.11** _____, hull and polish every grain of rice from a huge sack scattered all over the courtyard, and weed the rice paddies before the **8) 523.8** _____ come out, paddies that spread out before her like a great green **9) 551.48** _____. But Pear Blossom is not alone. Three magical **10) 591** _____ assist her, a gigantic **11) 597.8** _____, a flock of **12) 598.2** _____ and a huge black ox. It is with the help of these creatures that Pear Blossom is able to attend the **13) 394.26** _____ and becomes a nobleman s wife.

Key: 1. Korea 2. magic 3. tree 4. sun 5. cook 6. water 7. apple 8. stars, 9. lake 10. animals 11. frog 12. birds 13. festival

TALES FROM ASIA AND INDIA

The Boy of the Three Year Nap by Diane Snyder. Illus. by Allan Say. Boston, Houghton-Mifflin, 1988.

Boy Who Drew Cats by Margaet Hodges. Illus. by Aki Sogabe. New York, Holiday, 2002.

Brave Little Parrot by Rafe Martin. Illus. by Susan Gaber. New York, Putnam, 1998.

The Crane Wife by Odds Bodkin. Illus. by Genady Spirin. San Diego, Harcourt Brace, 1998.

The Donkey and the Rock by Demi. New York, Holt, 1999.

The Empty Pot by Demi. New York, Holt, 1990.

Foolish Rabbit's Big Mistake by Rafe Martin. Illus. by Ed Young. New York, Putnam, 1985.

The Gift of the Crocodile: A Cinderella Story by Judy Sierra. Illus. by Reynold Ruffins. New York, Simon & Schuster, 2000.

Lord of the Cranes by Kerstin Chen. Illus. by Jian Jiang. New York, North-South, 2000.

Momotaro, the Peach Boy by Linda Shute. New York, Lothrop, 1986.

The Rabbit's Tale: A Tale from Korea by Suzanne Han. Illus. by Richard Wehrman. New York, Holt, 1999.

The Silver Charm: A Tale from Japan by Robert San Suci. Illus. by Yoriko Ito. New York, Doubleday, 2002.

The Sun Girl and the Moon Boy by Yangsook Choi. New York, Knopf, 1997.

Tale of the Mandarin Ducks by Katherine Paterson. Illus. by Leo and Diane Dillon. New York, Lodestar, 1990.

Three Samurai Cats by Eric Kimmel. Illus. by Mordecai Gerstein. New York, Holiday House, 2003.

Two of Everything by Lily Toy Hong. Morton Grove, IL, Whitman, 1993.

Yeh Shen by Ai-Ling Louie. Illus. by Ed Young. New York, Philomel, 1982.

FOLKTALES FROM AFRICA

Tales Retold by Verna Aardema

Match the title with the tale.

1. _____ A young girl finds a magic shell that causes her to fall into the hands of a spirit. She must get free.

2. _____ This story tells about the dry lands of Africa and of the boy, Ki-Pat, who finds a way to make the dark cloud release the rain.

3. _____ This tale explains how the leopard gets its spots, and its comeuppance.

4. _____ Ananse always tricks another out of his money, until the cat helps out.

5. _____ The rat, the buck deer, and the lion fail to guard their home against a terrible creature, but the small tree toad succeeds.

6. _____ A boy saves a snake and in return the snake gives him the ability to understand animals.

7. _____ A play about a small creature who can't get into her house because Long One is inside and is threatening her.

The Tales:

A. *Vingananee and the Tree Toad*

B. *Who s In Rabbit's House?*

C. *Bimwili and the Zimwi*

D. *What's So Funny, Ketu?*

E. *Bringing the Rain to Kapiti Plain*

F. *Oh Kojo! How Could You!*

G. *Half-a-Ball-of-Kenki*

Key: 1. C 2. E 3. G 4. F 5. A 6. D 7. B

FOLKTALES FROM AFRICA

Solve the cryptograms to find titles of folktales from Africa.

The code:

A	B	C	D	E	F	G	H	I	J	K	L	M	N	O	P	Q	R	S	T	U	V	W	X	Y	Z
J	D	L	H	W	M	A	F	U	O	Q	V	B	I	R	N	Y	P	E	G	K	T	S	C	X	Z

1. J I J I W U H R W E G F W U B N R E E U D V W

   _____ _____ ____ _____

2. D U B S U V U J I H G F W E U B S U

   _____ ____ ____ _____

3. Q R U J I H G F W Q R V J I K G E

   ____ ____ ____ _____ _____

4. B U E R E R: R I L W K N R I J G U B W

   _____ _____ _____ __ _____

   G J V W E M P R B J M P U L J

   _____ _____ _____

5. P J D D U G B J Q W E J B R I Q W X

   _____ _____ __ _____

   R M V U R I

   ___ _____

6. S F R ' E U I P J D D U G ' E F R K E W

   _____,___ ____ _____,_____

7. S F X B R E Y K U G R W E D K C C U I

   ____ _____ ____ ___

   N W R N V W ' E W J P E W

   _____,___ _____

Key: 1. Anansi Does the Impossible 2. Bimwili and the Zimwi 3. Koi and the Kola Nuts 4. Misolo: Once Upon A Time Tales from Africa 5. Rabbit Makes A Monkey of Lion 6. Who's In Rabbit's House? 7. Why Mosquitoes Buzz in People's Ears

FOLKTALES FROM AFRICA

Choose the Right Word

Mufaro's Beautiful Daughters, written and illustrated by John Steptoe. Scholastic, 1987

Help tell this booktalk by choosing the best word to complete each statement.

1. Mufaro had two daughters. Nyasha was caring and courteous but Manyara was disagreeable and

   A) altruistic   B) generous   C) rapacious

2. The king wished to choose a wife so he began a search for a woman who was

   A) hideous   B) exquisite   C) unattractive

3. Manyara left the village long before the others hoping to be the first to see the

   A) monarch   B) despot   C) dictator

4. She was unkind to those she met along the way and treated them

   A) humanely   B) ruthlessly   C) graciously

5. When Nyasha set out, she stopped to help those in need, She was

   A) self-centered   B) barbarous   C) compassionate

6. As Nyasha neared the palace, Manyara met her and said that something terrible was waiting in the king's chamber! It was

   A) repulsive   B) captivating   C) amiable

7. Although Nyasha was frightened by her sister's words, she anxiously opened the door and entered the chamber. She was

   A) confident   B) apprehensive   C) assured

   Then she smiled at what she saw. Can you guess the happy ending to this tale?

Key: 1. C 2. B 3. A 4. B 5. C 6. B 7. B

From *Books Every Child Should Know: The Literature Quiz Book* by Nancy Polette. Westport, CT: Libraries Unlimited. Copyright © 2006.

FOLKTALES FROM AFRICA

The Adventures of Spider: West African Folk Tales by Joyce Arkhurst. Illus. by Jerry Pinkney. Boston, Little-Brown, 1964.

Ananse and the Lizard by Pat Cummings. New York, Holt, 2002.

Anansi Does the Imposible: An Ashanti Tale by Verna Aardema. Illus. by Lisa Desimini. New York, Atheneum, 1997.

Bimwili and the Zimwi by Verna Aardema. Illus. by Susan Medaugh. New York, Dial, 1985.

The Hat Seller and the Monkeys: A West African Folk Tale by Baba Diakite. New York, Scholastic, 1999.

How Many Spots Does A Leopard Have? by Julius Lester. Illus. by David Shannon. New York, Scholastic, 1989.

In the Rainfield: Who Is the Greatest? by Isaac Olaleye. Illus. by Ann Grifalconi. New York, Scholastic, 2002.

Jabuti the Tortoise by Gerald McDermott. San Diego, Harcourt, 2001.

Koi and the Kola Nuts by Verna Aardema. Illus. by Joe Cepeda. New York, Atheneum, 1999.

The Magic Gourd by Baba Diakite. New York, Scholastic, 2003.

Misoso: Once Upon A Time Tales from Africa by Verna Aardema. Illus. by Reynolds Ruffins. New York, Knopf, 1994.

Rabbit Makes A Monkey of Lion by Verna Aardema. Illus. by Jerry Pinkney. New York, Dial, 1989.

Who's In Rabbit's House? by Verna Aardema. Illus. by Leo and Diane Dillon. New York, Dial, 1977.

Why Mosquitoes Buzz In People's Ears by Verna Aardema. Illus. by Leo and Diane Dillon. New York, Dial, 1975.

Zomo, the Rabbit: A Trickster Tale from West Africa by Gerald McDermott. San Diego, Harcourt Brace, 1992.

HISPANIC FOLKTALES AND FAIRYTALES

Solve the cryptogram and discover the titles of ten Hispanic tales.

The code:

A	B	C	D	E	F	G	H	I	J	K	L	M	N	O	P	Q	R	S	T	U	V	W	X	Y	Z
F	R	U	J	M	Y	T	S	W	N	B	Z	D	Q	P	G	I	C	L	V	H	K	E	O	A	X

1. F J M Z W V F

   _____

2. R P C C M T H W V F   F Q J   V S M   U P A P V M

   _____   _____   _____   _____

3. V S M   T P Z J   U P W Q

   _____   _____   _____

4. W L F R M Z Z M   F Q J   V S M   S H Q T C A

   _____   ____   ____   _____

   U P A P V M

   _____

5. N H F Q   R P R P   T P M L   V P   E P C B

   _____   _____   _____   ___   _____

6. N H L V   F   D W Q H V M

   _____   __   _____

7. Z W V V Z M   T P Z J   L V F C

   _____   ____   _____

8. L Z M M G W Q T   R C M F J

   _____   _____

9. L M Q P C   U F V ' L   C P D F Q U M

   _____   _____   _____

10. V F Z M L   Y C P D   L W Z K M C   Z F Q J L

    _____   ____   _____   _____

Key: 1. Adelita 2. Borreguita and the Coyote 3.The Gold Coin 4. Isabelle and the Hungry Coyote 5. Juan Bobo Goes To Work 6. Just A Minute 7. Little Gold Star 8. Sleeping Bread 9. Senor Cat's Romance 10. Tales from Silver Lands

A Mexican Folktale Adapted by Nancy Polette

SCAVENGER HUNT

Visit your library shelves to find the topic for each Dewey number below. Write the topic on the line after the number. Read the story.

Jose Martinez lived in the **1) 728.8** _____ of the **2) 909** _____. When the king heard about a princess with a golden smile he sent Jose on a journey to seek her out. Day after day he rode his **3) 636.1** _____ across the disty plains. He traveled over **4) 551.4** _____ and across **5) 574.5** _____. With the help of an eagle, a **6) 598.2** _____, and a small **7) 597** _____, Jose finds the princess and takes her to the **8) 909** _____. The princess is upset to find that the king is very old. She vows that there will be no wedding until he sends someone to fetch **9) 551.48** _____ from the Magic Waterfall. Away Jose goes, traveling through dark and dangerous **10) 577.3** _____. At last he finds the Magic Waterfall and brings back water from it. Before drinking the **11) 551.48** _____ himself, the king orders Jose to be killed, then sprinkled with the **12) 551.48** _____ to see if it will bring him back to life. Jose dies and the princess proceeds to sprinkle Jose with the **13) 551.48** _____ from a small **14) 639.412** _____ bottle. Will the **15) 551.48** _____ bring him back to life? If it does, will the princess have to keep her promise and marry the **16) 909** _____? It is Jose she truly loves. What will she do?

Key: 1. palace 2. king 3. horse 4. mountains 5. deserts 6. dove or birds 7. fish 8. king 9. water 10. forest 11. water 12. water 13. water 14. pearl 15. water 16. king

HISPANIC FOLKTALES AND FAIRYTALES: TITLE GAME

Here are first lines from seven Hispanic folktales. Unscramble the titles below and write the title under the first line that best fits.

1. The ghostly image floating in the night air transformed itself into a bat.

   _____

2. Juan Pobreza, the blacksmith, lived on the pampas. His name suited him perfectly because pobreza means *poverty* in Spanish.

   _____

3. Juan has been a thief for many, many years, so many, in fact, that he can't even remember what it's like to be anything else.

   _____

4. This is the tale of the village of San Pedro and of two men who were important to the life of that town.

   _____

5. By sparing the life of the Water Spirit, Tambo, Chancay proved himself kind and worthy.

   _____

6. Borreguita, the little ewe lamb, was eating lush plants in the meadow when the coyote came along.

   _____

7. On a night when the wind howled through the trees and the rain cried tears in protest, Maya was born.

   _____

A. amyas dnreiclh
B. het eiepngls daerb
C. gibarouret dna het oeycto
D. het tab
E. yacnhac dna het trcese fe ifer
F. het dlog nioc
G. hbtliamcsk dna het vidle

Key: 1. The Bat (D) 2. The Blacksmith and the Devil (G) 3. The Gold Coin (F) 4. The Sleeping Bread (B) 5. Chancay and the Secret of Fire (E) 6. Borreguita and the Coyote (C) 7. Maya's Children (A)

HISPANIC FOLKTALES AND FAIRY TALES

Adelita: A Mexican Cinderella Story by Tomie De Paola. New York, Putnam, 2002

Borreguita and the Coyote, A Tale from Mexico by Verna Aardema. New York, Knopf, 1991.

Chancay and the Secret of Fire by Donald Charles. New York, Putnam's, 1992.

The Gold Coin by Alma Flor Ada. New York, Aladdin Books, 1994.

Golden Tales by Lulu Delacre. New York, Scholastic, 1996.

Isabelle and the Hungry Coyote by Keith Polette. Illus. by Esther Szegedy. Minneapolis, Raven Tree, 2004.

Jabuti, the Tortoise: A Trickster Tale from the Amazon by Gerald McDermott. New York, Harcourt, 2001.

Juan Bobo Goes to Work by Marisa Montes. Illus. by Joe Cepeda. New York, HarperCollins, 2000.

Just A Minute: A Trickster Tale and Counting Book by Yuyi Morales. San Francisco, Chronicle Books, 2003.

The Little Gold Star by Robert San Souci. Illus. by Sergio Martinez. New York, HarperCollins, 2000.

Mexican Ghost Tales of the Southwest by Alfred Avila, Austin, TX, Piñata Books 1994.

Musicians of the Sun by Gerald McDermott. New York, Simon & Schuster, 1997.

The Rooster Who Went to His Uncle's Wedding by Alma Flor Ada. Illus. by Kathleen Kuchera. New York, Putnam, 1993.

Señor Cat's Romance and Other Favorite Stories from Latin America retold by Lucia Gonzalez. New York, Scholastic, 1997.

The Sleeping Bread by Stefan Czernecki and Timothy Rhodes. New York, Hyperion, 1992.

Tale of Rabbit and Coyote by Tony Johnston. Illus. by Tomie de Paola. New York, Putnam, 1994.

AMERICAN TALL TALES

Solve the cryptograms to discover nine American tall-tale heroes and heroines.

The code:

A B C D E F G H I J K L M N O P Q R S T U V W X Y Z
A N S W B Q R G Z U F E P D H K X J O M C I V Y T L

1. U H G D D T   A K K E B O B B W

   _____   _____

2. K A C E   N C D T A D

   _____   _____

3. U H B   P A R A J A S

   _____   _____

4. O A E E T   A D D   M G C D W B J

   _____   _____   _____

5. U H G D   G B D J T

   _____   _____

6. W A I T   S J H S F B M M

   _____   _____

7. H E W   O M H J P A E H D R

   _____   _____

8. O P H F T   P H C D M A Z D   J H O B

   _____   _____   _____

9. O M B A P N H A M   A D D Z B

   _____   _____

Key: 1. Johnny Appleseed 2. Paul Bunyan 3. Joe Magarac 4. Sally Ann Thunder 5. John Henry 6. Davy Crockett 7. Old Stormalong 8. Smoky Mountain Rose 9. Steamboat Annie

From *Books Every Child Should Know: The Literature Quiz Book* by Nancy Polette. Westport, CT: Libraries Unlimited. Copyright © 2006.

AMERICAN TALL TALES: WORD SEARCH

Find and circle the last name of each tall-tale hero or heroine.

n	m	a	g	a	r	a	c
a	y	a	y	p	e	d	c
y	k	r	n	p	d	j	r
n	j	a	n	l	n	s	o
u	r	o	f	e	u	o	c
b	t	i	n	s	h	d	k
a	n	r	l	e	t	u	e
k	e	n	e	e	s	d	t
e	r	d	t	d	t	e	t

1. Joe_____

2. Casey _____

3. Mike _____

4. Sally Ann_____

5. John _____

6. Paul_____

7. Johnny_____

8. Davy _____

Key: 1. Magarac 2. Jones 3. Fink 4. Thunder 5. Henry 6. Bunyan
7. Appleseed 8. Crockett

From *Books Every Child Should Know: The Literature Quiz Book*
by Nancy Polette. Westport, CT: Libraries Unlimited. Copyright © 2006.

AMERICAN TALL TALES: SCAVENGER HUNT

Visit the library shelves to find the topic for each Dewey number. Write the topic on the line after each number. Read the booktalks.

A. *Sally Ann Thunder Ann Whirlwind Crockett*, retold and illustrated by Steven Kellogg. Morrow, 1995.

Who was the toughest living creature in all the old **1) 978.0049** _____? Why, none other than Sally Ann Thunder Ann Whirlwind. On the day she was born she could out-talk, out-grin, out-scream, out-**2) 797.21** _____ and out-run any baby in **3) 976.9** _____. Within a few years she was more than a match for bears, rattlers, **4) 597.98** _____, and even the mighty Mike Fink. She so stunned a **5) 599.7446** _____ with her grin that he rolled over backwards and skinned himself on the rocks. But when Sally Ann rescued Davy Crockett from a pair of rampaging **6) 598.943** _____ by lassoing six rattlers together to make a lariat, even her hornet's nest bonnet and skunk perfume didn't stop him from proposing **7) 392.5** _____.

B. *Swamp Angel* by Anne Isaacs. Illus. by Paul O. Zelinsky. Dutton, 1994.

When Angelica Longrider was born, she was scarcely taller than her mother and couldn't climb a **1) 582.16** _____ without help. She was a full two years old before she built her first **2) 694.2** _____. But by the time she was fully grown, Swamp Angel, as she was known, could lasso a **3) 551.553** _____ and drink an entire **4) 551.482** _____ dry. She single-handedly saved the settlers from the fearsome **5) 599.7446** _____ known as Thundering Tarnation, wrestling him from the top of the Great Smoky **6) 551.432** _____ to the bottom of a deep lake. It was a fight that lasted five days. When both Swamp Angel and the bear were too tired to fight, they went to sleep and Swamp Angel's snores were so loud that she snored down a huge **7) 582.16** _____ which landed on the bear and killed it. Swamp Angel paid tribute to her foe and then had enough bear meat to feed everyone in **8) 917.68** _____.

Key: A.1. frontier 2. swim 3. Kentucky 4. alligator 5. bear 6. eagles
7. marriage
B.1. tree 2. log cabin 3. tornado 4. lake 5. bear 6. mountains
7. tree 8. Tennessee

AMERICAN TALL TALES: NAME THE HERO

Name that tall-tale hero! Match the description with the hero's name.

1. _____ Bossed a team of lumberjacks in the North Woods and ate half a wagonload of potatoes for lunch. His pet was a blue ox.

2. _____ Raised by coyotes and made the first lasso by squeezing poison from a rattlesnake.

3. _____ Grew up in the Connecticut Valley, moved west with the settlers, and wore a hat made from a cook pot.

4. _____ Born from an ore pit. Used hands to mix molten steel. Melted himself down to create a new steel mill.

5. _____ Died winning a contest with a steam engine to drill a tunnel through a mountain.

6. _____ Train engineer who died saving the lives of others.

7. _____ The strongest man on the Mississippi River.

8. _____ Could beat her brothers at any sport. Saved the life of Davy Crockett and married him.

9. _____ Killed a bear when he was three. Rode on a bolt of lightning to escape a tornado on the Mississippi River.

10. _____ Ship's captain who fashioned England's White Cliffs of Dover with soap.

A. Davy Crockett   F. Joe Magarac
B. Old Stormalong   G. Sally Ann Thunder Ann Whirlwind Crockett
C. John Henry   H. Pecos Bill
D. Casey Jones   I. Mike Fink
E. Paul Bunyan   J. Johnny Appleseed

Key: 1. E 2. H 3. J 4. F 5. C 6. D 7. I 8. G 9. A 10. B

AMERICAN TALL TALES

American Tall Tales by Adrien Stoutenberg. Illus. by Richard M. Powers. New York, Penguin, 1976.

American Tall Tales by Mary Pope Osborne. Illus. by Michael McCurdy. New York, Knopf, 1991.

Cut from the Same Cloth: American Women of Myth, Legend and Tall Tales by Robert San Souci. Illus. by Brian Pinkney. New York, Philomel, 1993.

Davy Crockett Saves the World by Rosalyn Schanzer. New York, HarperCollins, 2001.

John Henry by Ezra Jack Keats. New York, Pantheon, 1965.

John Henry Illus. by Jerry Pinkney. New York, Dial, 1994.

Johnny Appleseed by Steven Kellogg. New York, Morrow, 1988.

Larger than Life: The Adventures of American Legendary Heroes by Robert San Souci. Illus. by Andrew Glass. New York, Doubleday, 1991.

Ol' Paul, the Mighty Logger by Glen Rounds. New York, Holiday House, 1949.

Paul Bunyan by Steven Kellogg. New York, Morow, 1986.

Paul Bunyan by Esther Shephard. San Francisco, Harcourt, 1985.

Pecos Bill by Steven Kellogg. New York, Morrow, 1986.

Sally Ann Thunder Ann Whirlwind Crockett. New York, Morrow, 1995.

Smokey Mountain Rose by Alan Schroeder. Illus. by Brad Sneed. New York, Dial, 1997.

Steamboat Annie and the Thousand Pound Catfish by Katherine Wright. Illus. by Howard Fine. New York, Philomel, 2001.

NATIVE AMERICAN TALES: MATCHING GAME

Match the description of each tale with its title.

1. How the first horses came to be as a gift from the Great Spirit to the Plains Indians.

2. A young boy must make a journey to the sun to remove the scar on his face.

3. An Indian girl delivers cloaks she has made to her seven brothers, thus creating the Big Dipper.

4. An Algonquin girl has a scarred face from tending the fire, but is the only one in the village who can see the magnificent Invisible Being.

5. Four men receive pouches from Gluskabe, but are warned not to open them until they reach home. Three disobey and the fourth finds an empty pouch.

6. A boy longs for two lives, one in the world of people and the other, in an ocean home with the seals.

7. After angering the bears, a young girl of the Raven Clan is kidnapped by them and forced to be their servant.

8. A blind boy is left behind when his tribe moves to a summer fishing camp, but Mouse Woman comes to the rescue.

9. When the last of the Indian tribes were defeated and the final treaties signed, Chief Seattle, head of the Northwest Nations, spoke to those who wished to buy the Indian lands.

10. A young hunter must pass several tests before he can join his wife in the Buffalo Nation.

A. ____ Buffalo Woman   F. ____ Seal Oil Lamp

B. ____ Her Seven Brothers   G. ____ Star Boy

C. ____ Rough Face Girl   H. ____ Gluskabe and the Four Wishes

D. ____ Gift of the Sacred Dog I. ____ Girl Who Lived with Bears

E. ____ Brother Eagle, Sister Sky J. ____ Boy Who Lived with Seals

Key: A. 1   B. 3   C. 4   D. 1   E. 9   F. 8   G. 2   H. 5   I. 7   J. 6

NATIVE AMERICAN TALES

Choose the Right Word

Circle the best word to complete each sentence below. Read the story.

1. Long ago all the fire on earth was hoarded by two old women. They were

   A) covetous   B) considerate   C) unselfish   D) altruistic

2. The women refused the hungry animals who tried to buy the fire. The animals felt

   A) blissful   B) mellow   C) vulnerable   D) gratified

3. The animals asked coyote to help secure the fire. They knew he was very

   A) amiable   B) benevolent   C) savage   D) competent

4. Coyote told the animals to station themselves along the way to pass the firebrand from one to another. This would be an animal

   A) relay   B) consortium   C) rally   D) conclave

5. Chased by the women, each animal seized the firebrand in turn, running

   A) happily   B) frantically   C) impatiently   D) sporadically

6. The last to receive the firebrand was frog. He could not run fast. The women were near. Frog felt

   A) pathetic   B) overwhelmed   C) amused   D) optimistic

7. Frog swallowed the firebrand and dove into the river. The fire in his throat made frog feel

   A) weary   B) dejected   C) ridiculous   D) afflicted

8. Frog spat the firebrand out on pieces of wood. However, the fire had burned his throat so to this day Frog has a voice that is

   A) melodious   B) raspy   C) obsolete   D) benign

Key: 1. A   2. C   3. D   4. A   5. B   6. B   7. D   8. B

NATIVE AMERICAN TALES

Scavenger Hunt

Visit the library shelves to find the topic for each Dewey number in the booktalks. Write the topics on the lines after each number.

The First Strawberries, retold by Joseph Bruchac

How was it that **1) 635.75** _____ came into the world? This is how: Long ago when the world was new the creator made a man and a woman. They **2) 392.5** _____ and for a long time lived together and were happy. Yet one day the couple quarreled and the woman left the man in **3) 152.4** _____ and haste. To stop the woman's flight the **4) 523.7** _____ sent to **5) 550** _____ raspberries, then blueberries, then blackberries. But only the sun's final gift of **6) 634.75** _____ had the power to reunite the couple. And to this day they are a reminder that **7) 302.34** _____ and respect are as sweet as the taste of ripe, red berries.

Coyote Places the Stars by Harriet Peck Taylor

One evening crafty **8) 599.77** _____ climbs to the **9) 523.3** _____ to discover the secrets of the **10) 523.1** _____. Instead he finds a way to make the most wonderful **11) 758.9** _____ for all the world to see. When the other **12) 591** _____ of the **13) 551.442** _____ look up at the sky the next **14) 525.35** _____ they are in for a big surprise, in this tale of the origin of the **15) 523.8** _____.

> Key: 1. strawberries 2. married 3. anger 4. sun 5. Earth 6. strawberries 7. friendship 8. coyote 9. moon 10. universe 11. pictures 12. animals 13. canyon 14. night 15. constellations

NATIVE AMERICAN TALES

Arrow to the Sun by Gerald McDermott. New York, Viking, 1974.

Boy Who Lived with Bears and other Iroquois Stories by Joseph Bruchac. Illus. by Murv Jacob. New York, HarperCollins, 1995.

Boy Who Lived with the Seals by Rafe Martin. Illus. by David Shannon. New York, Putnam, 1993.

Brother Eagle, Sister Sky: A Message From Chief Seattle. Paintings by Susan Jeffers. New York, Dial Books for Young Readers, 1991.

Buffalo Woman by Paul Goble. New York, Bradbury, 1984.

Coyote, A Trickster Tale from the American Southwest by Gerald McDermott. SanDiego, Harcourt Brace, 1994.

Coyote Places the Stars by Harriet Peck Taylor. New York, Bradbury, 1993.

The First Strawberries: A Cherokee Story by Joseph Bruchac. Illus. by Anna Vojtech. New York, Dial, 1993.

Gift of the Sacred Dog by Paul Goble. New York, Bradbury, 1980.

Girl Who Loved Wild Horses by Paul Goble. New York, Bradbury, 1978.

Gluskabe and the Four Wishes by Joseph Bruchac. Illus. by Christine Shraeder. New York, Cobblehill, 1995.

Her Seven Brothers by Paul Goble. New York, Bradbury, 1988.

Iktomi and the Berries by Paul Goble. New York, Orchard, 1989.

The Legend of the Bluebonnet by Tomie De Paola. New York, Putnam, 1983.

The Loon's Necklace by William Toye. Illus. by Elizabeth Cleaver. Cambridge, Oxford University Press, 1977.

Lord of the Animals: A Miwok Indian Creation Myth by Fiona French. Brookfield, CT, Millbook, 1997.

The Lost Children by Paul Goble. New York, Bradbury, 1993.

The Mud Pony by Caron Lee Cohen. Illus. by Shonto Begay. New York, Scholastic, 1988.

Raven, A Trickster Tale from the Pacific Northwest by Gerald McDermott. New York, Penguin, 1975.

The Seal Oil Lamp by Dale DeArmond. Boston, Little Brown, 1988.

Sootface: An Ojibwa Cinderella by Robert San Souci. Illus. by Daniel San Souci. New York, Doubleday, 1994.

Star Boy by Paul Goble. New York, Bradbury, 1993.

THE CLASSICS WORD SEARCH

Complete the last word in the titles below. Circle the word in the word search.

i	s	l	a	n	d	r	i
s	s	n	n	e	m	o	w
e	b	o	r	d	r	a	w
h	r	s	r	r	r	h	i
o	w	n	p	a	n	o	l
o	r	i	b	g	o	o	l
d	m	b	o	z	k	p	o
b	i	o	o	o	n	l	w
t	o	r	k	d	i	h	s

1. The Wind in the _____
2. Swiss Family _____
3. Peter _____
4. Jungle _____
5. Secret _____
6. Little _____
7. The Lion, the Witch, and the _____
8. Peter _____
9. Winnie the _____
10. Robin _____
11. Treasure _____

Key: 1. Willows 2. Robinson 3. Pan 4. Book 5. Garden 6. Women
7. Wardrobe 8. Rabbit 9. Pooh 10. Hood 11. Island

From *Books Every Child Should Know: The Literature Quiz Book*
by Nancy Polette. Westport, CT: Libraries Unlimited. Copyright © 2006.

THE CLASSICS: HIDDEN TITLES

Underline fourteen different classic literature titles hidden in this story.

There once was a little prince who fell in love with a little princess named Beauty. Before they could marry, a wicked witch captured Beauty. The witch's name was Alice. In wonderland she had a castle where she kept Beauty prisoner. Beauty's prison was covered with thick vines like a jungle. Book after book was given to her to pass the time but she read very little. Women were hired by the witch to see to her every comfort. The witch dressed her in gowns made of velveteen. Rabbit fur was sewn into a soft cloak for her. Still she was sad.

The little prince undertook an incredible journey to find Beauty. On the way he battled a strong wind. In the willows his horse refused to go on. The water had turned black. Beauty was in danger. But the prince knew the witch's secret. Garden flowers tossed in the castle window would release Beauty from the spell. First he asked the Borrowers for flowers but they had none.Then he asked his friends Heidi and Pinocchio but they had no flowers. Finally he went to his friend Tom's midnight garden and gathered as many flowers as he could carry. When he reached the castle where the little princess was held captive, he threw the flowers in the window and released the spell. They married and lived happily ever after.

Key: 1. Little Prince 2. Little Princess 3. Alice In Wonderland 4. Jungle Book 5. Little Women 6. Velveteen Rabbit 7. Incredible Journey 8. Wind in the Willows 9. Black Beauty 10. Secret Garden 11. Borrowers 12. Heidi 13. Pinocchio 14. Tom's Midnight Garden

---

CLASSICS QUIZ

A Classic Tales Quiz

1. How many *Little Women* were there?
   A) six   B) two   C) four

2. What did *Peter Pan* lose?
   A) his cap   B) his shadow   C) his kite

3. In the *Wizard of Oz*, what did the Wicked Witch of the West fear most?
   A) fire   B) wild animals   C) water

4. Who did the *Little Princess* want to find?
   A) her friend   B) her father   C) her mother

5. The main character in *The Secret Garden* is
   A) Mary   B) Sarah   C) Martha

6. To get to Wonderland, Alice fell down
   A) a ladder   B) some stairs   C) a rabbit hole

7. The man who carved the puppet, *Pinocchio*, was named
   A) Gepetto   B) Alfonse   C) Pierre

8. Mrs. Pepper, a widowed mother, had how many children?
   A) two   B) five   C) ten

9. The Robinson family from Switzerland were
   A) kidnapped   B) imprisoned   C) shipwrecked

10. Tom Sawyer's aunt was named
    A) Aunt Jane   B) Aunt Polly   C) Aunt Emily

11. Hans Brinker's sister's name was
    A) Sally   B) Gertrude   C) Gretel

12. *Heidi* lived with
    A) her grandfather   B) her mother   C) her older sister

13 *Winnie the Pooh's* friend Eeyore is a
    A) dog   B) rabbit   C) donkey

14) *The Wind in the Willows* tells the adventures of
    A) Ted, Tim, and Mike   B) Dog, Cat, and Rat   C) Mole, Rat, and Toad

continued on next page

CLASSICS QUIZ

(continued)

15. *Peter Rabbit* ran and hid from Farmer
    A) McCandle   B) McGregor   C) McCarthy

16. *Mary Poppins* took Jane and Michael to visit her Uncle
    A) Charles   B) Oddkins   C) Wigg

17. *The Borrowers* live
    A) in an attic   B) beneath a kitchen floor   C) in a bank

18. The boy who visited a midnight garden was named
    A) Tom   B) Michael   C) Jack

19. In *The Jungle Book*, the boy raised by wolves was named
    A) Chandu   B) Mowgli   C) Abbah

20. *The Incredible Journey* is made by
    A) three deer   B) two dogs and a cat   C) two cats

21. In *Treasure Island*, Long John Silver was
    A) a pirate   B) a ship's captain   C) a ship's doctor

22. The oldest toy in the nursery was
    A) the Velveteen Rabbit   B) the Rag Doll   C) the Skin Horse

23. *The Little Prince* owned
    A) a precious jewel   B) a beautiful flower   C) a magic cloak

24. *The Pied Piper of Hamelin* rid the town of
    A) roaches   B) rats   C) mosquitoes

25. *Robin Hood's* sworn enemy was
    A) Prince Charles   B) The King of England   C) the Sheriff of Nottingham

26. *Black Beauty was*
    A) a Great Dane   B) a leopard   C) a horse

Key: 1. C 2. B 3. C 4. B 5. A 6. C 7. A 8. B 9. C 10. B 11. C 12. A 13. C 14. C 15. B 16. C 17. B 18. A 19. B 20. B 21. A 22. C 23. B 24. B 25. C 26. C

THE CLASSICS

A *Wind in the Willows* Quiz

Circle the letters as directed.

1. If Toad liked music, circle the letter B; if not, circle the letter L.

2. If mole was a poet, circle T; if not, circle O.

3. If Toad Hall was built of yellow brick, circle N; if not, circle I.

4. If Toad went from one fad to another, circle S; if not, circle N.

5. If the caravan was wrecked because the horse was frightened by a bee, circle L; if not, circle T.

6. If rat was Toad's enemy, circle M; if not, circle E.

7. If Toad kept house himself, circle Z; if not, circle R.

8. If Mole liked to paint, circle O; if not, circle K.

9. If Toad had a terrible temper, circle S; if not, circle U.

10. If all three animals were frightened by a motor car, circle L; if not, circle S.

List the circled letters in order on the lines below.

The word spelled by the circled letters will describe Toad's personality:

—— —— —— —— —— —— —— —— —— ——

Word: boisterous

From *Books Every Child Should Know: The Literature Quiz Book*
by Nancy Polette. Westport, CT: Libraries Unlimited. Copyright © 2006.

THE CLASSICS

The Call of the Wild by Jack London, 1903

Classic Scavenger Hunt

Visit the library shelves. Find the topic for each Dewey number. Write the topic on the line after the matching number to complete the booktalk.

The Call of the Wild by Jack London

The story begins with four-year-old Buck, a **1) 636.7** _____ who is half St. Bernard, leading a life of relative ease on Judge Miller's estate in **2) 979.4** _____. To pay off a **3) 795** _____ debt, Manuel, who takes care of the **4) 712.6** _____, sells Buck to two strangers, and the dog's troubles begin. He is taken to the **5) 917.19** _____ in the frozen North and beaten into submission as he is trained to become a sled dog. The instincts of his **6) 599.744** _____ ancestors emerge as Buck fights with the lead dog for the top spot in pulling the sled. Buck adapts to the severe **7) 551.6** _____ and hard workloads and begins to feel the call of the **8) 333.7** _____. When the team is sold to cruel masters, Buck is saved from a beating by John Thornton, who becomes his new master. Thornton treats Buck with kindness and the dog and man become firm **9) 177.6** _____. They travel far into the Alaskan wilderness in search of **10) 553.41** _____ and Thornton meets his death on the trip. Buck, rather than returning to civilization, joins a pack of **11) 599.744** _____, submitting himself completely to the call of the wild.

Key: 1. dog 2. California 3. gambling 4. gardens 5. Yukon 6. wolf 7. weather 8. wilderness 9. friends 10. gold 11. wolves

THE CLASSICS: SCAVENGER HUNT

The Secret Garden by Frances Hodgson Burnett, Knopf, 1988

Visit the library shelves to find the topic for each Dewey number below. Write the topics on the lines after the matching number.

Mary Lennox lived with her parents in **1) 594** _____. Those who knew Mary well, like her nurse, disliked her thoroughly. She was always demanding or scowling. She would not hesitate to kick a **2) 636.8** _____ if it got in her way. Her hair was wild and stringy like the wild **3) 582.13** _____ that grew on the moors.

On this particular morning Mary was vexed as usual. Her nurse had not come to dress her. No matter that the old nurse might have been caring throughout the night for victims of disease caused by terrible **4) 616.9** _____. Sickness had swept through **5) 594** _____ like the plague. It was killing young and old alike.

The hours passed. Now, one might think a nine-year-old could put on her **6) 646** _____ and find some **7) 612.3** _____, but not Mary. She did not know how. Finally, after a very long time, the door to her room flew open and there stood a very surprised-looking British officer.

The officer shook his head in disbelief and mumbled to himself. "We will have to send her by **8) 387.2** _____ to whatever family she has left in **9) 942** _____. She is an orphan now. I wonder who will care for her?"

The answer to that question is what this book is all about, for Mary is sent to live in her Uncle's great lonely house on the English moors—a house filled with secrets.

Key: 1. India 2. cat 3. flowers 4. germs 5. India 6. clothes 7. food 8. boat 9. England

CHILDREN'S CLASSICS: AN ANNOTATED LIST

Alcott, Louisa. *Little Women.* New York, Little-Brown, 1968 (1868). The joys and sorrows of four sisters during the Civil War.

Barrie, J. M. *Peter Pan.* New York, Buccaneer Books, 1980 (1911). Three children fly to Never-Never Land with Peter Pan, a boy who refuses to grow up.

Baum, Frank L. *The Wizard of Oz.* New York, Holt, 1982 (1900). Dorothy is carried by a cyclone to the Land of Oz, where she discovers both friendship and danger.

Burnett, Frances H. *The Secret Garden.* New York, Harper & Row, 1987 (1909). Mary finds a hidden garden and helps a young boy to regain his health.

Burnford, Sheila. *The Incredible Journey.* Boston, Little Brown, 1961. A cat and two dogs meet and overcome many dangers in their travels.

Carroll, Lewis. *Alice's Adventures In Wonderland.* New York, Knopf, 1988 (1865). Alice falls down a rabbit hole to find a land of unusual people.

Collodi, Carol. *The Adventures of Pinocchio.* New York, Knopf, 1988 (1883). A wooden puppet learns the hard way what it takes to become a real boy.

Dodge, Mary. *Hans Brinker.* New York, Scholastic, 1988 (1865). A boy in Holland wins silver skates.

Graham, Kenneth. *The Wind in the Willows.* New York, Scribners, 1983 (1908). Mole, Rat, and Badger often pay for friend Toad's enthusiasms.

Irving, Washington. *Rip Van Winkle.* New York, New American Library, 1961 (1819). Rip has a twenty-year sleep and many surprises when he awakens.

Kipling, Rudyard. *Just-So Stories.* New York, Grossett & Dunlap, 1950 (1902). How various animals got specific characteristics.

Lewis, C. S. *The Lion, the Witch, and the Wardrobe.* New York, MacMillan, 1950. Four children find adventure in the strange land of Narnia.

Lindgren, Astrid. *Pippi Longstocking.* New York, Viking, 1950. A super-strong little girl with a horse for a friend.

Lofting, Hugh. *The Voyages of Doctor Doolittle.* New York, Delacorte, 1988 (1920). A doctor discovers he can talk to animals.

London, Jack. *Call Of the Wild.* New York, Macmillan, 1963 (1903). The dog, Buck, is stolen, taken north, and becomes leader of a wild pack.

continued on next page

From *Books Every Child Should Know: The Literature Quiz Book* by Nancy Polette. Westport, CT: Libraries Unlimited. Copyright © 2006.

CHILDREN'S CLASSICS: AN ANNOTATED LIST (continued)

Milne, A. A. *Winnie the Pooh*. New York, Dutton, 1988 (1926). The adventures of Christopher Robin, Pooh, and Piglet.

Montgomery, Lucy Maud. *Anne of Green Gables*. New York, Bantam, 1976 (1904). Her adoptive parents don't know quite what to make of lively Anne.

Pyle, Howard. *Robin Hood*. Los Angeles, Dover, 1968 (1803). An outlaw of Sherwood Forest robs the rich to pay the poor.

Saint-Exupéry, Antoine de. *The Little Prince*. New York, Harcourt, 1943. A small prince leaves his planet and discovers wisdom.

Salten, Felix. *Bambi*. New York, Simon & Schuster, 1928. A young deer faces many dangers while growing up.

Sewel, Anna. *Black Beauty*. New York, Grosset, 1945 (1877). A horse is rescued from a cruel master.

Spyri, Johanna. *Heidi*. New York, Puffin, 1990 (1881). Heidi is sent to live with a grandfather she has never met.

Travers, P. C. *Mary Poppins*. New York, Harcourt, 1934. Mary Poppins proves to be a most unusual nanny to the Banks children.

Twain, Mark. *The Adventures of Huckleberry Finn*. New York, Scholastic, 1982 (1885). *The Adventures of Tom Sawyer*. New York, Morrow, 1989 (1876). Adventure stories of two boys living in the Midwest the mid-1800s.

White, E. B. *Charlotte's Web*. New York, Harper & Row, 1952. Charlotte the spider finds an unusual way to save Wilbur the pig from the butcher.

Wilder, Laura Ingalls. *Little House in the Big Woods*. New York, Harper & Row, 1952 (1932). Frontier life in a loving family during the 1870s.

Williams, Margery. *The Velveteen Rabbit*. New York, Knopf, 1985 (1922). A velveteen rabbit must learn how to become real.

From *Books Every Child Should Know: The Literature Quiz Book*
by Nancy Polette. Westport, CT: Libraries Unlimited. Copyright © 2006.

FANTASY TITLES

Find and circle the missing word in each title below in the fantasy word search.

n	r	t	o	h	h	e	n	i
r	i	e	c	i	m	m	g	h
w	s	a	k	i	w	n	i	s
y	e	l	t	t	i	l	q	n
p	r	b	k	k	l	u	u	i
y	c	o	m	p	a	s	s	u
i	e	u	t	r	w	e	g	g
h	i	n	e	c	r	o	w	n
a	n	e	d	r	a	g	m	e
e	w	o	n	k	g	f	n	p

1. Grey _____

2. Charlie & the Chocolate _____

3. Kneeknock _____

4. James & the Giant _____

5. Mr. Popper's _____

6. Cricket in Times _____

7. Children of Green _____

8. Rabbit _____

9. Enormous _____

10. Wrinkle in _____

11. Mrs. Frisby & the Rats of _____

12. The Hero & the _____

13. Tom's Midnight _____

14. The Golden _____

15. Charlotte's _____

16. Stuart _____

Key: 1. King 2. Factory 3. Rise 4. Peach 5. Penguins 6. Square 7. Knowe 8. Hill 9. Egg 10. Time 11. NIMH 12. Crown 13. Garden 14. Compass 15. Web 16. Little

FANTASY: IN WHICH STORY?

Place the number of each story before the pair of characters appearing in that story.

1. *Alice in Wonderland*
2. *Wizard of Oz*
3. *Charlie and the Chocolate Factory*
4. *The Phantom Tollbooth*
5. *The Whipping Boy*
6. *Kneeknock Rise*
7. *The Bad Beginning*
8. *The Lion, the Witch, and the Wardrobe*
9. *The High King*

10. *Charlotte's Web*
11. *Rabbit Hill*
12. *Mrs. Frisby and the Rats of NIMH*
13. *The Wind in the Willows*
14. *Pinocchio*
15. *The Borrowers*
16. *The Hobbit*
17. *Harry Potter series*
18. *The Indian in the Cupboard*

A. ____ Taran, Hen Wen
B. ____ Scarecrow, Tin Woodman
C. ____ Mad Hatter, White Rabbit
D. ____ Templeton, Wilbur
E. ____ Charlie Bucket, Willie Wonka
F. ____ Arrietty, Pod
G. ____ Water Rat, Mole
H. ____ Gepetto, Blue Fairy
I. ____ Nicodemus, Justin

J. ____ Bilbo, Gandalf
K. ____ Hermione, Ron
L. ____ Omri, Little Bear
M. ____ Georgie, Uncle Analdas
N. ____ Aslan, Snow Queen
O. ____ Klaus, Violet
P. ____ Milo, King Azoz
Q. ____ Jemmy, Prince Brat
R. ____ Megrimum, Egan

Key: A. 9 B. 2 C. 1 D. 10 E. 3 F. 15 G. 13 H. 14 I. 12 J. 16 K. 17 L. 18 M. 11 N. 8 O. 7 P. 4 Q. 5 R. 6

A FANTASY QUIZ

Write the letter of each book title on the line following its description.

A. *The Borrowers*

B. *The Cricket in Times Square*

C. *Dark Is Rising*

D. *Dragonsong*

E. *The High King*

F. *The Hobbit*

G. *The Indian in the Cupboard*

H. *James and the Giant Peach*

H. *The Lion, the Witch, and the Wardrobe*

J. *Mouse and His Child*

K. *The Phantom Tollbooth*

L. *Tuck Everlasting*

M. *The Whipping Boy*

N. *The Wind in the Willows*

O. *Wizard of Earthsea*

1. A pigkeeper must rescue a princess. _____

2. A cricket sings opera. _____

3. A family guards a magical spring. _____

4. A toad buys a motor car. _____

5. A boy seeks King Arthur's grail. _____

6. A cupboard brings toys alive. _____

7. A toy mouse and a dump rat. _____

8. Tiny people cook soup in a thimble. _____

9. A boy hides in the London sewers. _____

10. A boy visits the Mountains of Ignorance. _____

11. A school teaches magic. _____

12. A witch brings eternal winter. _____

13. A girl hides with fire dragons. _____

14. A grasshopper the size of a dog. _____

15. Giant spiders hold their prisoners in webs. _____

> Key: 1. E 2. B 3. L 4. N 5. C 6. G 7. J 8. A 9. M 10. K 11. O 12. H
> 13. D 14. H 15. F

SCAVENGER HUNT

Stuart Little by E.B. White, Harper & Row, 1945

Visit the library shelves to find the topic for each Dewey number below. Write each topic on the line after its number. Read the booktalk.

My name is Stuart Little. You can measure my **1) 531** _____ in ounces for I am very, very small. I am a **2) 599.32** _____ but I live in a human family. Being as small as I am does create some problems. To turn on a **3) 535** _____ I have to shinny up a cord. My bed is a matchbox, and washing up is no easy task. But I can also be very helpful. When my mother's ring went down the drain, guess who was the only one small enough to recover it? The **4) 728** _____ I live in is very large. Naturally I have to be careful. There was the time I used the ring on the shade as a trapeze. When the shade flew up to the top of the window with a loud snap, there I was rolled up in it with no way to escape. When I was finally rescued, who did I see staring at me, showing her sharp teeth but Snowball, the **5) 636.8** _____!

One morning we found a tiny **6) 639.9** _____ almost frozen to death on the windowsill. We thawed her out and she became my best **7) 155.4** _____. I protected her from Snowball, but there was no way to keep her safe from all the other neighborhood cats. When she found a note that said "Beware of a strange **8) 636.8** _____ who will come by night," she flew north as fast as she could fly. That left only one thing for me to do . . . go and find her. I left home without telling anyone. I thought I would be back soon . . . little was I to know that I might never ever return. I will need to send my family a **9) 759** _____ of my travels.

> Key: 1. weight 2. mouse 3. light 4. house 5. cat 6. bird 7. friend 8. cat
> 9. picture

SCAVENGER HUNT

Pippi Longstocking by Astrid Lindgren, Viking, 1950

Visit the library shelves to find the topic for each Dewey number below. Write the topics on the lines after the matching number. Read the booktalk.

My name is Annika and I want to tell you about my very strange **1) 155.4** _____ Pippi Longstocking. For a long time my brother Tommy and I wished someone would move in the empty **2) 728** _____ next door, but we never dreamed it would be someone our age with *no* parents to look after her. Pippi is different! She wears strange **3) 646** _____ and super-big shoes, and keeps her **4) 636.1** _____ on the porch because she says she doesn't want him in the kitchen and he doesn't like the parlor. When she wants to ride him, she just lifts him off the porch and away they go. When the **5) 363** _____ came to take her to the children's home, she led them up to the roof, then took away the ladder! When thieves awoke her in the middle of the night along with Mr. Nilsson, her pet **6) 599.8** _____ who sleeps in a tiny bed beside her, she was not at all alarmed. She taught them to **7) 793.3** _____ and gave each of them **8) 332.4** _____. Yes, Pippi is different, but that is what makes adventures with her so much fun. You never know what will happen next. Oh, I hear her calling. We are going to play with Pippi's **9) 625.1** _____ today. It's just like having a personal toy shop when Pippi is your next door neighbor.

Key: 1. friend 2. house 3. clothes 4. horse 5. police 6. monkey 7. dance
8. money 9. trains

SCAVENGER HUNT

Matilda by Roald Dahl, Puffin Books, 1972

Visit the library shelves to find the topic for each Dewey number below. Write the topics on the lines after the matching number. Read the booktalk.

Matilda did not exactly have an ideal **1) 306.8** _____. Her father sold stolen **2) 629.222** _____. Mrs. Wormwood spent her days playing bingo. Because she never got home until late, she did not do any **3) 641.5** _____, so the family had supper on a tray in front of the **4) 791.45** _____.

Matilda spoke clearly at the age of one and went to the **5) 027.8** _____ by herself at the age of four. Were the Wormwoods pleased with their child's unusual abilities? Of course not!

Matilda did not go to **6) 370.9** _____ until age five and a half because her parents forgot to enroll her. Her teacher was the smiley, huggy Miss Honey. It did not take Miss Honey long to discover how gifted Matilda was. Matilda could do even the most difficult **7) 510** _____ in her head.

Miss Trunchbull, the headmistress, told Miss Honey that Matilda could not possibly be a genius. Matilda's father had made it clear that the **8) 305.23** _____ was nothing but trouble.

Miss Trunchbull hated all children. She often talked about starting the ideal school . . . one with no children. So Matilda, Miss Honey and all the other students wished she would take off on a long **9) 629.13** _____ trip. Otherwise, it would take a superhuman genius to get rid of her. And that, of course, is exactly what Matilda was . . . a sweet, gentle—and crafty—genius!

> Key: 1. family 2. cars 3. cooking 4. television 5. library 6. school
> 7. math 8. child 9. balloon

From *Books Every Child Should Know: The Literature Quiz Book*
by Nancy Polette. Westport, CT: Libraries Unlimited. Copyright © 2006.

SCAVENGER HUNT

The BFG by Roald Dahl, Farrar, Straus & Giroux, 1982

Visit the library shelves to find the topic for each Dewey number below. Write the topics on the lines after the matching number. Read the booktalk.

Sophie trembled in fright. Inside the **1) 551.4** _____ it was as dark as night. The giant who had snatched her while she was **2) 154.6** _____ gently lowered her to the floor. Suddenly a blaze of **3) 535** _____ lit up the cavern.

"Please don't eat me," Sophie begged.

"I am not a cannybull," the giant shouted, I only eat "snozcumbers and other **4) 635** _____."

"Why did you steal me out of my bed?" Sophie asked.

"Because, you poor little scrumplet, you saw me out of your window. You would have told everyone that giants exist in places other than **5) 398.2** _____. We simply can't have that so you will just have to stay with me for the rest of your life. Don't worry, I'll protect you from the bad giants."

"What bad giants?" Sophie asked.

"The ones that eat little **6) 155.4** _____," said the BFG. "Human beans and especially little children are like strawbunkles and cream to those giants. Here, have a nice drink of frobscottle."

The more Sophie learns about the other horrible giants who guzzle little children all over the **7) 591.9** _____, the more she is determined to stop their guzzling. With the help of the BFG and a lot of **8) 623.7** _____ Sophie cooks up and carries out her plan. To find out how it all happens, read The BFG!

> Key: 1. cave 2. sleeping 3. light 4. vegetables 5. fairy tales 6. children 7. world 8. airplanes

FANTASY: HIDDEN TITLES

Underline hidden titles of fantasy tales by Lloyd Alexander.

The remarkable journey of Prince Zen began when all the stories in the Kingdom of Gobbaleen disappeared. The only book that had not been stolen was a book of three stories told over and over again by the gypsy Rizka. After many months of hearing the same stories, Prince Zen was determined to find the story thief and bring the stories back to Gobbaleen.

Prince Zen consulted the kingdom's best fortune tellers. They told him the stories had been stolen by a beggar. Queen Una, Prince Zen's mother, said there had never been a beggar in the house. Gobbaleen was a kingdom without beggars.

Prince Zen made his way to the land of the Arkadians. He found one called Gawgon stirring a black cauldron with a huge spoon. Gawgon and the boy who stood next to him had heard nothing about the stolen stories. Gawgon told Prince Zen to find Taran. Wanderer that he was, Taran might have heard news about the missing stories. When Prince Zen found Taran he also found the lost stories. Taran had heard a rumor that the gypsy Rizka had stolen them all. Prince Zen raced back to Gobbaleen and stormed the gypsy's caravan. Sure enough, the stories were in a large trunk secured by an iron ring. Prince Zen broke the ring with his magic sword and the first story he lifted out of the trunk was his favorite story, How the Cat Swallowed Thunder. Now the citizens of Gobbaleen are happy once more, for they can hear a different story every day.

Key:

The Arkadians. Dutton, 1995.

The Beggar Queen. Doubleday, 1984.

The Black Cauldron. Holt, 1965.

The Book of Three. Holt, 1964.

The Fortune-Tellers. Dutton, 1992.

The Gawgon and the Boy. Dutton, 2001.

The Gypsy Rizka. Dutton, 1999.

The High King. Dutton, 1968.

The House Gobbaleen. Dutton, 1999.

How the Cat Swallowed Thunder. Dutton, 1999.

The Iron Ring. Dutton, 1991.

The Remarkable Journey of Prince Zen. Dutton, 1991.

Taran Wanderer. Holt, 1999.

FANTASY: SYNONYM TITLES

Here are titles of popular fantasy tales, with many of the words in each title replaced by synonyms. On the line below each title, write the actual title.

Example:

1. The Elevated Monarch
    The High King
    _____

2. A Permanent Fold
    _____

3. A Destitute of Light Immediately Ascending
    _____

4. The Native American Enclosed in a Case for Dishes
    _____

5. The Small Rodent and His Offspring
    _____

6. A Small Enclosure for Money Collection Occupied by an Apparition
    _____

7. A Tome in Triplet
    _____

8. The Feline Desiring to Become a *Homo Sapien*
    _____

9. The Unrelenting Stannic Combatant
    _____

10. An Ovum of Gigantic Proportions
    _____

11. Elevations Totally Without Color
    _____

12. One of Masculine Gender Enduring Lashes
    _____

FANTASY: SYNONYM TITLES: KEY

1. *The High King* by Lloyd Alexander. New York, Henry Holt, 1968.

2. *Tuck Everlasting* by Natalie Babbitt. New York, Farrar, Straus & Giroux, 1975.

3. *The Dark is Rising* by Susan Cooper. New York, Atheneum, 1973.

4. *The Indian in the Cupboard* by Lynne Reid Banks. New York, Doubleday, 1981.

5. *The Mouse and His Child* by Russell Hoban. New York, Harper & Row, 1967.

6. *The Phantom Tollbooth* by Norton Juster. New York, Random House, 1961.

7. *The Book of Three* by Lloyd Alexander. New York, Henry Holt, 1964.

8. *The Cat Who Wished to Be A Man* by Lloyd Alexander. New York, E. P. Dutton, 1973.

9. *The Steadfast Tin Soldier* by Hans Christian Andersen. Retold by Lori Seidler. New York, HarperCollins, 1993.

10. *The Enormous Egg* by Oliver Butterworth. Boston, Little Brown, 1956.

11. *The White Mountains* by John Christopher. New York, Macmillan, 1971.

12. *The Whipping Boy* by Sid Fleischman. New York, Greenwillow, 1996.

SELECTED FANTASY: A BOOK LIST

Alexander, Lloyd. *The High King.* New York, Holt, 1968. Taran is an orphan hero, an assistant pig keeper in the Land of Prydain who must destroy the Black Cauldron and rescue Princess Eilonwy before he becomes the High King.

Babbitt, Natalie. *Tuck Everlasting.* New York, Farrar, Straus & Giroux, 1975. Violence erupts when the Tuck family discover that their secret about a spring that brings immortality has been discovered.

Banks, Lynne Reid. *The Indian in the Cupboard.* New York, Doubleday, 1981. A magical cupboard turns toys into living things.

Cooper, Susan. *The Dark is Rising.* New York, Atheneum, 1973. Will Stanton discovers on his 11th birthday that he's no ordinary British boy. He and his friends set of on an exciting quest to find King Arthur's grail, touching off a struggle between the forces of dark and light.

Dahl, Roald. *James and the Giant Peach.* New York, Knopf, 1961. In escaping his wicked aunts, a young boy finds strange new worlds.

Hoban, Russell. *The Mouse and His Child.* New York, Harper & Row, 1967. A wind-up toy mouse and his child, broken and then mended, set out to find the animals and doll house they had known in the toy shop. Along the way, they make enemies with a dump rat and have many adventures.

Juster, Norton. *The Phantom Tollbooth.* New York, Random House, 1961. When Milo receives a tollbooth as a gift, he finds that it admits him to a land where many adventures take place.

LeGuin, Ursula. *Wizard of Earthsea.* New York, Parnassus, 1968. A boy loses his parents, discovers he has magical powers, goes to a school that teaches magic, makes a best friend and an arch enemy, and battles the forces of evil as he grows up.

Lewis, C.S. *The Lion, the Witch, and the Wardrobe.* New York, Macmillan, 1961. Four English school children find their way through the back of a wardrobe into the magical land of Narnia and assist Aslan, the golden lion, to triumph over the White Witch, who has cursed the land with eternal winter.

McCaffrey, Anne. *Dragonsong.* New York, Atheneum, 1978. Forbidden by her father to indulge in music in any way, Menolly runs away, taking refuge with the fire dragons that open up a whole new world for her.

Selden, George. *The Cricket in Times Square.* New York, Farrar, Straus & Giroux, 1960. A Connecticut cricket is transported in a picnic basket to New York's Times Square.

SELECTED CALDECOTT WINNER TITLES 1940–59

Titles of books that have won the Caldecott Medal are listed below. Find the words listed in bold print in each title in the word search and circle them.

w	n	a	s	m	d	n	l	s	l
l	i	o	n	k	o	l	w	l	w
o	t	p	h	e	s	o	i	c	o
t	r	e	e	c	l	c	n	h	o
d	u	c	k	l	i	n	g	s	c
n	o	s	a	e	r	i	s	r	r
a	c	w	c	e	e	l	c	u	o
l	s	i	d	s	s	p	x	w	w
s	n	n	n	i	c	u	e	o	s
i	o	o	l	s	u	l	o	r	f
w	w	h	r	b	e	a	r	h	s

Abraham **Lincoln**

Song of the **Swallows**

Many **Moons**

The Biggest **Bear**

The Little **Island**

A Tree is **Nice**

Make Way for **Ducklings**

The Egg **Tree**

Prayer for a **Child**

White Snow, Bright **Snow**

The Little **House**

Finders **Keepers**

The Rooster **Crows**

The Frog Went A-**Courtin'**

Time of **Wonder**

Madeline's **Rescue**

The Big **Snow**

Chanticleer and the **Fox**

SELECTED CALDECOTT TITLES 1960–83

Titles of books that have won the Caldecott Medal are listed below. Find the words listed in bold print in each title in the word search and circle them.

n	a	m	m	o	u	s	e	f
u	c	d	e	v	i	l	n	f
s	h	i	p	a	b	h	i	o
e	r	o	m	b	n	o	h	h
a	i	s	e	l	h	r	s	d
m	s	p	g	w	h	s	n	u
c	t	t	o	n	g	e	o	l
y	m	m	o	a	i	s	o	u
d	a	y	y	r	r	k	m	z
n	s	d	f	e	y	k	d	s

Nine Days Till **Christmas**

Baboushka and the Three **Kings**

Once A **Mouse**

Where the Wild Things **Are**

The Funny Little **Woman**

Always Room for One **More**

Drummer **Hoff**

The Snowy **Day**

Duffy and the **Devil**

The Fool of the World and the Flying **Ship**

Sylvester and the Magic **Pebble**

A Story, A **Story**

The Girl Who Loved Wild **Horses**

May I Bring A **Friend**?

Arrow to the **Sun**

Ashanti to **Zulu**

Sam Bangs and **Moonshine**

Noah's **Ark**

From *Books Every Child Should Know: The Literature Quiz Book*
by Nancy Polette. Westport, CT: Libraries Unlimited. Copyright © 2006.

SELECTED CALDECOTT TITLES 1984–2004

Titles of books that have won the Caldecott Medal are listed below. Find the words listed in bold print in each title in the word search and circle them.

n	o	o	m	b	g	i	w	s	a
g	b	a	b	l	g	s	i	r	a
t	n	e	d	i	s	e	r	p	s
a	h	i	n	e	m	a	e	g	o
o	g	g	r	t	h	g	i	l	f
c	r	p	i	p	l	p	r	o	w
r	x	e	p	n	s	e	l	r	h
e	j	o	u	r	n	e	y	i	i
v	d	r	a	g	o	n	o	a	t
o	r	a	b	b	i	t	l	d	e

The Glorious **Flight**

Officer Buckle and **Gloria**

Hey **Al**

So You Want to be **President**

Lon Po **Po**

Mirette on the High **Wire**

Snowflake **Bentley**

Owl **Moon**

Smoky **Night**

The Polar **Express**

Joseph Had a Little **Overcoat**

The Oxcart **Man**

My Friend **Rabbit**

Grandfather's **Journey**

St. George and the **Dragon**

The Three **Pigs**

Black and **White**

From *Books Every Child Should Know: The Literature Quiz Book* by Nancy Polette. Westport, CT: Libraries Unlimited. Copyright © 2006.

A CALDECOTT QUIZ

1. Who did MEI LI want to meet at midnight?

    A) Santa Claus   B) the kitchen god   C) her mother

2. (Circle yes or no.) ABRAHAM LINCOLN by the d'Aulaires, tells of his assassination.

    A) yes   B) no

3. In THEY WERE STRONG AND GOOD, Robert Lawson tells about his

    A) home   B) work   C) ancestors

4. MAKE WAY FOR DUCKLINGS takes place in

    A) New York City   B) Boston   C) Atlanta

5. THE LITTLE HOUSE moved because of too many

    A) animals   B) birds   C) buildings

6. The princess in MANY MOONS is helped by a

    A) gooseherd   B) fairy   C) court jester

7. In PRAYER FOR A CHILD, what surrounds the first word on each page?

    A) flowers   B) angels   C) nothing

8. All the rhymes and jingles in THE ROOSTER CROWS are from what country?

    A) United States   B) England   C) Mexico

9. THE LITTLE ISLAND is visited by

    A) a bird   B) a cat   C) a deer

10. WHITE SNOW, BRIGHT SNOW shows the reactions to the snow of

    A) birds   B) children   C) clouds

11. In THE BIG SNOW, how many people help the birds and animals?

    A) three   B) six   C) two

12. The location of SONG OF THE SWALLOWS is

    A) Mexico   B) California   C) Hawaii

13. THE EGG TREE describes a custom that came from what country?

    A) Holland   B) Switzerland   C) Spain

continued on next page

A CALDECOTT QUIZ (continued)

14. The main characters in FINDERS KEEPERS are

    A) two children   B) farm animals   C) two dogs

15. THE BIGGEST BEAR is caught by a boy named

    A) Eddie   B) Al   C) Johnny

16. Who rescued MADELINE?

    A) a policeman   B) a fireman   C) a dog

17. Marcia Brown won the Caldecott for illustrating a Cinderella tale from

    A) Spain   B) France   C) Germany

18. In FROG WENT A-COURTIN', who did Frog marry?

    A) a butterfly   B) a mouse   C) Miss Frog

19. (Circle true or false.) A small tree is teased by its neighbors in A TREE IS NICE.

    A) true   B) false

20. TIME OF WONDER begins with what kind of weather in the woods?

    A) sunshine   B) fog   C) snow

21. What kind of animal is Chanticleer in CHANTICLEER AND THE FOX?

    A) pig   B) horse   C) rooster

22. NINE DAYS TO CHRISTMAS takes place in what country?

    A) United States   B) England   C) Mexico

23. Who does Baboushka welcome into her modest hut?

    A) three women   B) three doves   C) three kings

24. In ONCE A MOUSE, before the hermit transformed him the tiger was a

    A) cat   B) snake   C) dog

25. In THE SNOWY DAY, where does Peter live?

    A) on a farm   B) in the city   C) on an island

26. The main character in WHERE THE WILD THINGS ARE is named

    A) Chuck   B) Al   C) Max

27. In MAY I BRING A FRIEND? a hippo puts a foot in a

    A) pie   B) cake   C) pot of soup

continued on next page

A CALDECOTT QUIZ (continued)

28. ALWAYS ROOM FOR ONE MORE is based on a folk ballad from what country?

    A) England   B) Ireland   C) Scotland

29. In SAM BANGS AND MOONSHINE, how does Sam's father earn a living?

    A) as a fisherman   B) as a policeman   C) as a doctor

30. What did DRUMMER HOFF do at the end of the book?

    A) fired the cannon   B) went to sleep   C) joined the army

31. In FOOL OF THE WORLD AND THE FLYING SHIP, how many companions did the fool have?

    A) eight   B) three   C) two

32. In SYLVESTER AND THE MAGIC PEBBLE, what does Sylvester meet in the meadow?

    A) a rabbit   B) a lion   C) a turtle

33. A STORY, A STORY takes place where?

    A) India   B) Mexico   C) Africa

34. In ONE FINE DAY what does the fox steal from the old woman?

    A) milk   B) a pie   C) her shawl

35. THE FUNNY LITTLE WOMAN had a magical

    A) rice paddle   B) lamp   C) spinning wheel

36. In DUFFY AND THE DEVIL, the name that Duffy must guess is

    A) Rumpleboots   B) Snatchacatch   C) Tarraway

37. In ARROW TO THE SUN, a boy goes on a journey to find

    A) his brother   B) his sister   C) his father

38. In WHY MOSQUITOES BUZZ IN PEOPLE'S EARS, what does iguana have in his ears?

    A) dirt   B) leaves   C) sticks

39. What kind of picture book is ASHANTI TO ZULU?

    A) a counting book   B) a story book   C) an ABC book

continued on next page

A CALDECOTT QUIZ (continued)

40. In NOAH'S ARK, what does the dove bring to Noah?

    A) an olive branch   B) a palm leaf   C) a small fish

41. THE GIRL WHO LOVED WILD HORSES becomes lost in a

    A) forest   B) storm   C) maze

42. The OX-CART MAN made a journey to what city?

    A) Portsmouth   B) Boston   C) New York

43. (Circle yes or no.) Arnold Lobel won the Caldecott Award for illustrating Aesop's Fables.

    A) yes   B) no

44. In JUMANJI, the girl in the story is named

    A) Mary   B) Judy   C) Betsy

45. SHADOW takes place in what part of the world?

    A) Spain   B) Africa   C) Australia

46. THE GLORIOUS FLIGHT was undertaken by what famous aviator?

    A) Berliot   B) Earhart   C) Lindbergh

47. In SAINT GEORGE AND THE DRAGON, St. George married Princess

    A) Marissa   B) Una   C) Katherine

48. What does the boy lose in THE POLAR EXPRESS?

    A) money   B) a toy train   C) a bell

49. In HEY, AL, what is Al's dog's name?

    A) Fido   B) Eddie   C) Rex

50. The number of human characters in OWL MOON is:

    A) four   B) none   C) two

51. The SONG AND DANCE MAN was the children's

    A) grandfather   B) father   C) uncle

52. In LON PO PO, who does the wolf pretend to be?

    A) a friend   B) a relative   C) a neighbor

53. How many stories are told in BLACK AND WHITE?

    A) three   B) four   C) two

continued on next page

A CALDECOTT QUIZ (continued)

54. What animals fly on the second TUESDAY evening?

    A) pigs   B) monkeys   C) birds

55. In MIRETTE ON THE HIGH WIRE, who does Mirette help?

    A) a sick dog   B) a man   C) her mother

56. In GRANDFATHER'S JOURNEY, Grandfather began his journey in

    A) Japan   B) United States   C) China

57. In SMOKY NIGHT a young boy is worried about his missing

    A) money   B) football   C) cat

58. OFFICER BUCKLE AND GLORIA learn the value of

    A) money   B) safety   C) working together

59. In THE GOLEM, a rabbi created a huge clay

    A) man   B) lion   C) bird

60. (Circle true or false.) Zelinsky's RAPUNZEL was illustrated with woodcuts.

    A) true   B) false

61. In what state does SNOWFLAKE BENTLEY take place?

    A) Missouri   B) Vermont   C) Maryland

62. What was the last item that JOSEPH made from his little overcoat?

    A) a scarf   B) a handkerchief   C) a story

63. In SO YOU WANT TO BE PRESIDENT, how many presidents were born in log cabins?

    A) nine   B) six   C) none

64. In Weisner's THREE PIGS, how are the pigs able to fly?

    A) they grow wings   B) with paper airplanes   C) by magic

65. In MY FRIEND RABBIT, what gets stuck in a tree?

    A) a cat   B) an airplane   C) a kite

66. In what country were the towers the man walked between?

    A) United States   B) England   C) France

67. Where was the last place kitten went on KITTEN'S FIRST FULL MOON?

    A) the forest   B) the porch   C) beside the lake

KEY FOR THE CALDECOTT QUIZ

1. B	23. C	45. B
2. B	24. C	46. A
3. C	25. B	47. B
4. B	26. C	48. C
5. C	27. B	49. B
6. C	28. C	50. C
7. B	29. A	51. A
8. A	30. A	52. B
9. B	31. A	53. B
10. B	32. B	54. B
11. C	33. C	55. B
12. B	34. A	56. B
13. A	35. A	57. C
14. C	36. A	58. C
15. C	37. C	59. A
16. C	38. C	60. B
17. B	39. C	61. B
18. B	40. C	62. C
19. B	41. A	63. A
20. B	42. B	64. B
21. C	43. A	65. B
22. C	44. B	66. A
		67. B

A CALDECOTT STORY

Underline the titles of thirteen Caldecott Medal winners in this story.

Once a mouse decided to visit a little island. There was no one on the island to play with, so he invited Officer Buckle and Gloria to visit. "May I bring a friend?" Officer Buckle asked.

"There is always room for one more on this island," the mouse replied. "Just the other day, Noah's ark with all the animals of the Bible stopped by for tea. Just don't go walking the forest where the wild things are. A tree is nice, but the forest can be dangerous."

It was only nine days to Christmas and the mouse wanted to see some white snow. "Bright snow would be wonderful," he said. Officer Buckle told mouse that life on an island can be a time of wonder, but not to expect a big snow. Mouse forgot about the snow and built a fire. Late on that smoky night he listened while Officer Buckle told him a story. A story is a wonderful way to end a day, mouse thought, as he drifted off to sleep.

Key: Once A Mouse, Little Island, Officer Buckle and Gloria, May I Bring A Friend?, Always Room for One More, Noah's Ark, Animals of the Bible, Where the Wild Things Are, A Tree is Nice, Nine Days to Christmas, White Snow, Bright Snow, Time of Wonder, A Story, A Story

---

CALDECOTT SETTINGS

Write the letter of each state or country before the Caldecott title to show where the story took place. Some settings will be used more than once.

1. _____ Mei Li		A. Africa
2. _____ Abraham Lincoln		B. California
3. _____ Make Way for Ducklings		C. China
4. _____ Song of the Swallows		D. Vermont
5. _____ Madeline's Rescue		E. Illinois
6. _____ Time of Wonder		F. France
7. _____ Nine Days to Christmas		G. Boston
8. _____ Fool of the World and the Flying ship		H. Mexico
9. _____ A Story, A Story		I. Russia
10. _____ Why Mosquitoes Buzz in People's Ears		J. Maine
11. _____ Shadow		K. Mexico
12. _____ The Glorious Flight		
13. _____ Lon Po Po		
14. _____ Smoky Night		
15. _____ Snowflake Bentley		

Key: 1. C 2. E 3. G 4. B 5. F 6. J 7. K 8. I 9. A 10. A 11. A 12. F 13. C 14. B 15. D

LIBRARY SCAVENGER HUNT

Visit the library shelves to find the topic for each Dewey number in the booktalk. Write each topic on the line after the matching number. Read the completed booktalk for this winner of the Caldecott Medal.

Grandfather's Journey by Allen Say, Houghton Mifflin, 1993.

A young man from **1) 952** _____ was amazed at the sights he

saw when he set forth to see the **2) 912** _____. In **3) 973**

_____ he rode boats and **4) 625.1** _____ and often

walked to see **5) 574.5** _____, the open fields, **6) 551.4** _____,

and busy **7) 307.7** _____.

When he returned to his homeland, he married and brought his bride to

the **8) 975** _____. But he never forgot **9) 952** _____, and when

his daughter was grown, he took his family to that country. They lived

there in a city until the war destroyed his **10) 690** ____, and the family

moved to a small village. When his grandson grew up, the boy traveled to

the United States and discovered that he had two homes—one in Japan

and one in **11) 979.4** _____. He loved both, and just like his

grandfather, when he was in one, he missed the other.

Key: 1. Japan 2. world 3. United States 4. trains 5. deserts
6. mountains 7. cities 8. United States 9. Japan 10. house
11. California

LIBRARY SCAVENGER HUNT

Visit the library shelves to find the topic for each Dewey number in the booktalk. Write each topic on the line after the matching number. Read the completed booktalk for this winner of the Caldecott Medal.

Hey, Al by Arthur Yorinks, Farrar, Straus & Giroux, 1986

Al, a poor janitor, lives in one room with his **1) 636.7** _____, Eddie. Eddie is tired of being poor and longs for a better life. He gets his wish when Al is visited by a large **2) 598** _____ who promises to take Al and Eddie to a **3) 793.8** _____ place where they can have all the **4) 332.4** _____ and treats they desire and where there is no **5) 331.7** _____. At first Al and Eddie enjoy the beautiful place where they can eat and drink and **6) 797.2** _____ whenever they wish. Then one day Al discovers that their noses are beginning to look like beaks—they are slowly turning into **7) 598** _____. After the two escape, Al believes that Eddie has drowned in the **8) 55.46** _____ and is very sad. But the two are eventually reunited and discover that **9) 177.6** _____ is the best gift of all.

Key: 1. dog 2. bird 3. magic 4. money 5. work 6. swimming 7. birds 8. ocean 9. friendship

From *Books Every Child Should Know: The Literature Quiz Book* by Nancy Polette. Westport, CT: Libraries Unlimited. Copyright © 2006.

LIBRARY SCAVENGER HUNT

Visit the library shelves to find the topic for each Dewey number in the booktalk. Write each topic on the line after the matching number. Read the completed booktalk for this winner of the Caldecott Medal.

My Friend Rabbit by Eric Rohmann, Roaring Brook Press, 2002

When **1) 636.088** _____ lets his best friend, Rabbit, play with his brand new **2) 387.7** _____, trouble isn't far behind. Rabbit means well but he is much bigger than Mouse, and when he tries to launch the plane it ends up in a tree, too high to reach.

Rabbit tells Mouse not to worry because he has an idea. Rabbit gathers together lots of **3) 591** _____ and gets them to climb on each other. A tall ladder of **4) 591** _____ results, with rhino on top of **5) 599.6** _____, hippo on top of rhino, antelope on top of hippo, **6) 567.9** _____ on top of antelope, bear on top of crocodile, goose on top of bear, and squirrel on top of goose holding **7) 636.088** _____. Reaching for the plane proves to be a disaster when the animal ladder collapses, sending the animals bouncing every which way. Mouse is left hanging onto the wing of the plane, which is still stuck in the **8) 582.16** _____.

Finally the plane is rescued, but trouble looms again when Rabbit tries to take a plane ride with mouse. This is a charming story of toys, trouble, and **9) 177.6** _____ and of having a bigger playmate.

Key: 1. mouse 2. airplane 3. animals 4. animals 5. elephants
6. crocodile 7. mouse 8. tree 9. friendship

CALDECOTT MEDAL WINNERS

2005: *Kitten's First Full Moon* by Kevin Henkes. New York, Greenwillow Books

2004: *The Man Who Walked Between the Towers* by Mordicai Gerstein. Brookfield, CT, Roaring Brook Press/Millbrook Press

2003: *My Friend Rabbit* by Eric Rohmann. Brookfield, CT, Roaring Brook Press/Millbrook Press

2002: *The Three Pigs* by David Wiesner. Boston, Clarion/Houghton Mifflin

2001: *So You Want to Be President?* by Judith St. George. Illustrated by David Small. New York, Philomel Books

2000: *Joseph Had a Little Overcoat* by Simms Taback. New York, Viking

1999: *Snowflake Bentley* by Jacqueline Briggs Martin. Illustrated by Mary Azarian. Boston, Houghton Mifflin

1998: *Rapunzel* by Paul O. Zelinsky. New York, E.P. Dutton

1997: *Golem* by David Wisniewski. Boston, Clarion

1996: *Officer Buckle and Gloria* by Peggy Rathmann. New York, Putnam

1995: *Smoky Night* by Eve Bunting. Illustrated by David Diaz. San Diego, Harcourt

1994: *Grandfather's Journey* by Allen Say. Edited by Walter Lorraine. Boston, Houghton Mifflin

1993: *Mirette on the High Wire* by Emily Arnold McCully. New York, Putnam

1992: *Tuesday* by David Wiesner. Boston, Clarion Books

1991: *Black and White* by David Macaulay. Boston, Houghton Mifflin

1990: *Lon Po Po: A Red-Riding Hood Story from China* by Ed Young. New York, Philomel

1989: *Song and Dance Man* by Karen Ackerman. Illustrated by Stephen Gammell. New York, Knopf

1988: *Owl Moon* by Jane Yolen. Illustrated by John Schoenherr. New York, Philomel

1987: *Hey, Al* by Arthur Yorinks. Illustrated by Richard Egielski. New York, Farrar

1986: *The Polar Express* by Chris Van Allsburg. Boston, Houghton Mifflin

1985: *Saint George and the Dragon,* retold by Margaret Hodges. Illustrated by Trina Schart Hyman. New York, Little Brown

1984: *The Glorious Flight: Across the Channel with Louis Bleriot* by Alice and Martin Provensen. New York, Viking

1983: *Shadow,* illustrated and translated by Marcia Brown, original text in French by Blaise Cendrars. New York, Scribner

1982: *Jumanji* by Chris Van Allsburg. Boston, Houghton Mifflin

1981: *Fables* by Arnold Lobel. New York, HarperCollins

1980: *Ox-Cart Man* by Donald Hall. Illustrated by Barbara Cooney. New York, Viking

1979: *The Girl Who Loved Wild Horses* by Paul Goble. New York, Bradbury

1978: *Noah's Ark* by Peter Spier. New York, Doubleday

1977: *Ashanti to Zulu: African Traditions* by Margaret Musgrove. Illustrated by Leo & Diane Dillon. New York, Dial

1976: *Why Mosquitoes Buzz in People's Ears* retold by Verna Aardema. Illustrated by Leo & Diane Dillon. New York, Dial

1975: *Arrow to the Sun* by Gerald McDermott. New York, Viking

1974: *Duffy and the Devil* retold by Harve Zemach. Illustrated by Margot Zemach. New York, Farrar

1973: *The Funny Little Woman* retold by Arlene Mosel. Illustrated by Blair Lent. New York, Dutton

1972: *One Fine Day,* retold and illustrated by Nonny Hogrogian. New York, Macmillan

1971: *A Story, A Story: An African Tale*, retold and illustrated by Gail E. Haley. New York, Atheneum

1970: *Sylvester and the Magic Pebble* by William Steig. New York, Windmill

1969: *The Fool of the World and the Flying Ship*, retold by Arthur Ransome. Illustrated by Uri Shulevitz. New York, Farrar

1968: *Drummer Hoff*, adapted by Barbara Emberley. Illustrated by Ed Emberley. New York, Prentice-Hall

1967: *Sam, Bangs & Moonshine* by Evaline Ness. New York, Henry Holt

1966: *Always Room for One More* by Sorche Nic Leodhas [pseud. Leclair Alger]. Illustrated by Nonny Hogrogian. New York, Henry Holt

1965: *May I Bring a Friend?* by Beatrice Schenk de Regniers. Illustrated by Beni Montresor. New York, Atheneum

1964: *Where the Wild Things Are* by Maurice Sendak. New York, HarperCollins

1963: *The Snowy Day* by Ezra Jack Keats. New York, Viking

1962: *Once a Mouse*, retold and illustrated by Marcia Brown. New York, Scribner

1961: *Baboushka and the Three Kings* by Ruth Robbins. Illustrated by Nicolas Sidjakov. Boston, Parnassus

1960: *Nine Days to Christmas* by Marie Hall Ets and Aurora Labastida. Illustrated by Marie Hall Ets. New York, Viking

1959: *Chanticleer and the Fox*, adapted from Chaucer's *Canterbury Tales* by Barbara Cooney. Illustrated by Barbara Cooney. New York, Crowell

1958: *Time of Wonder* by Robert McCloskey. New York, Viking

1957: *A Tree Is Nice* by Janice Udry. Illustrated by Marc Simont. New York, Harper & Row

1956: *Frog Went A-Courtin'*, retold by John Langstaff. Illustrated by Feodor Rojankovsky. New York, Harcourt

1955: *Cinderella, or the Little Glass Slipper*, illustrated and translated by Marcia Brown from the original by Charles Perrault. New York, Scribner

1954: *Madeline's Rescue* by Ludwig Bemelmans. New York, Viking

1953: *The Biggest Bear* by Lynd Ward. Boston, Houghton Mifflin

1952: *Finders Keepers* by Will [pseud. William Lipkind]. Illustrated by Nicolas [pseud. Nicholas Mordvinoff]. San Diego, Harcourt

1951: *The Egg Tree* by Katherine Milhous. New York, Scribner

1950: *Song of the Swallows* by Leo Politi. New York, Scribner

1949: *The Big Snow* by Berta and Elmer Hader. New York, Macmillan

1948: *White Snow, Bright Snow* by Alvin Tresselt. Illustrated by Roger Duvoisin. New York, Lothrop

1947: *The Little Island* by Golden MacDonald [pseud. Margaret Wise Brown]. Illustrated by Leonard Weisgard. New York, Doubleday

1946: *The Rooster Crows* by Maude and Miska Petersham. New York, Macmillan

1945: *Prayer for a Child* by Rachel Field. Illustrated by Elizabeth Orton Jones. New York, Macmillan

1944: *Many Moons* by James Thurber. Illustrated by Louis Slobodkin. New York, Harcourt

1943: *The Little House* by Virginia Lee Burton. Boston, Houghton Mifflin

1942: *Make Way for Ducklings* by Robert McCloskey. New York, Viking

1941: *They Were Strong and Good* by Robert Lawson. New York, Viking

1940: *Abraham Lincoln* by Ingri and Edgar Parin d'Aulaire. New York, Doubleday

1939: *Mei Li* by Thomas Handforth. New York, Doubleday

1938: *Animals of the Bible, A Picture Book*, text selected by Helen Dean Fish. Illustrated by Dorothy P. Lathrop. New York, Lippincott

NEWBERY MEDAL WINNERS 1922–42

Complete each title below. Find and circle the missing words in the word search.

o	s	o	a	a	l	w	r	r	g	i
k	n	w	a	l	d	o	o	w	d	u
r	h	e	s	r	o	e	u	n	c	s
a	e	s	c	i	l	t	i	e	e	
k	a	r	u	k	i	a	g	i	s	t
o	v	o	e	z	t	g	n	a	y	a
w	e	h	e	n	t	i	u	d	t	k
e	n	w	u	s	l	r	w	n	s	s
a	b	o	o	n	e	f	a	w	d	g
s	m	c	o	u	r	a	g	e	u	i
y	e	a	r	s	r	e	m	m	u	s
n	w	a	l	d	o	o	w	l	g	f

1. Voyages of Dr. _____
2. Waterless _____
3. The Dark _____
4. Yung Fu of the Upper _____
5. Tales from Silver _____
6. Invincible _____
7. Shen of the _____
8. Caddie _____
9. Smoky the _____
10. Roller _____

11. Gay _____
12. The White _____
13. Trumpeter of _____
14. Thimble _____
15. Hitty, Her First Hundred _____
16. Daniel _____
17. The Cat Who Went to _____
18. Call It _____
19. Matchlock _____

Key: 1. Doolittle 2. Mountain 3. Frigate 4. Yangtze 5. Lands 6. Louisa 7. Sea 8. Woodlawn 9. Cowhorse 10. Skates 11. Neck 12. Stag 13. Krakow 14. Summer 15. Years 16. Boone 17. Heaven 18. Courage 19. Gun

From *Books Every Child Should Know: The Literature Quiz Book*
by Nancy Polette. Westport, CT: Libraries Unlimited. Copyright © 2006.

NEWBERY MEDAL WINNERS 1922–42

Write the letter of each title before the matching description.

A. Voyages of Dr. Doolittle

B. Waterless Mountain

C. The Dark Frigate

D. Yung Fu of the Upper Yangtze

E. Tales from Silver Lands

F. Invincible Louisa

G. Shen of the Sea

H. Caddie Woodlawn

I. Smoky the Cowhorse

J. Roller Skates

K. Gay Neck

L. The White Stag

M. Trumpeter of Krakos

N. Thimble Summer

O. Hitty, Her First Hundred Years

P. Daniel Boone

Q. The Cat Who Went to Heaven

R. Call It Courage

S. Matchlock Gun

T. Dobry

1. _____ Stories from all over South America.

2. _____ A busy man tries to learn the language of shellfish.

3. _____ Sixteen stories that capture Chinese traditions.

4. _____ Young Phil is forced to join a band of pirate thieves.

5. _____ A stolen herd, vicious rustlers, and a wild bronco make an exciting tale.

6. _____ A family's home is burned to the ground. A horseman attempts to rob the family on the road. The year is 1461.

7. _____ A young boy finds a way to outsmart river bandits.

8. _____ A doll has many adventures, including meeting Charles Dickens.

9. _____ A pigeon delivers secret messages during a war.

10. _____ A cat helps an artist to paint the Buddha for a sacred temple.

11. _____ Younger brother learns how to be a medicine man.

12. _____ A young woman nurses soldiers during the Civil War and writes a book.

13. _____ A young boy is needed to tend the animals but longs to study art.

continued on next page

NEWBERY MEDAL WINNERS 1922–42 (continued)

Write the letter of each title before the matching description.

A. Voyages of Dr. Doolittle
B. Waterless Mountain
C. The Dark Frigate
D. Yung Fu of the Upper Yangtze
E. Tales from Silver Lands
F. Invincible Louisa
G. Shen of the Sea
H. Caddie Woodlawn
I. Smoky the Cowhorse
J. Roller Skates

K. Gay Neck
L. The White Stag
M. Trumpeter of Krakos
N. Thimble Summer
O. Hitty, Her First Hundred Years
P. Daniel Boone
Q. The Cat Who Went to Heaven
R. Call It Courage
S. Matchlock Gun
T. Dobry

14. _____ A tomboy prevents an Indian attack.

15. _____ In 1890, Lucinda meets a lot of people in New York City, unbeknownst to her aunts.

16. _____ Attila the Hun and his tribes follow a ghost horse westward.

17. _____ Garnet has a miserable summer until she finds a good luck charm.

18. _____ The story of one of America's earliest heroes, who settled Kentucky.

19. _____ The son of an island chief is afraid of the sea and must prove his courage.

Key: 1. E 2. A 3. G 4. C 5. I 6. M 7. D 8. O 9. K 10. Q 11. B 12. F 13. T 14. H 15. J 16. L 17. N 18. P 19. R

NEWBERY MEDAL WINNERS 1943–63

Complete each title below. Find and circle the missing words in the word search.

d	o	l	p	h	i	n	s	h
s	c	h	o	o	l	l	n	b
l	l	i	h	n	r	a	o	p
l	h	c	t	i	d	w	o	b
e	j	k	g	a	l	n	l	o
u	o	o	o	m	d	l	l	w
g	h	r	s	e	d	n	a	m
i	n	y	y	r	n	t	b	w
m	r	p	w	t	i	m	e	t
h	l	t	e	e	w	a	i	n

1. Adam of the _____

2. Secret of the _____

3. Johnny _____

4. And Now _____

5. Rabbit _____

6. Wheel on the _____

7. Strawberry _____

8. Carry On Mr. _____

9. Miss _____

10. Miracles on Maple _____

11. Twenty One _____

12. Rifles for _____

13. King of the _____

14. Witch of Blackbird _____

15. Door in the _____

16. Onion _____

17. Amos Fortune: Free _____

18. Island of the Blue _____

19. Ginger _____

20. Bronze _____

21. Wrinkle in _____

Key: 1. Road 2. Andes 3. Tremain 4. Miguel 5. Hill 6. School 7. Girl 8. Bowditch 9. Hickory 10. Hill 11. Balloons 12. Watie 13. Wind 14. Pond 15. Wall 16. John 17. Man 18. Dolphins 19. Pye 20. Bow 21. Time

NEWBERY MEDAL WINNERS 1943–63

Write the letter of each title before the matching description.

A. Adam of the Road
B. Secret of the Andes
C. Johnny Tremain
D. And Now Miguel
E. Rabbit Hill
F. Wheel on the School
G. Strawberry Girl
H. Carry On Mr. Bowditch
I. Miss Hickory
J. Miracles on Maple Hill
K. Twenty One Balloons

L. Rifles for Watie
M. King of the Wind
N. Witch of Blackbird Pond
O. Door in the Wall
P. Onion John
Q. Amos Fortune: Free Man
R. Island of the Blue Dolphins
S. Ginger Pye
T. Bronze Bow
U. Wrinkle in Time

1. _____ In thirteenth century England a boy's dog is stolen and his father disappears.

2. _____ After a boy's hand is badly injured, he becomes a spy for the Sons of Liberty.

3. _____ A small animal is hit by a car but then cared for by humans.

4. _____ A family tries to survive in wild, unsettled Florida.

5. _____ A doll made from a twig worries that a squirrel might eat her nut head.

6. _____ Professor Sherman takes off to see the world in a most unusual way.

7. _____ A beloved colt soon becomes a bag of bones.

8. _____ Robin has lost the use of his legs but longs to become a knight.

9. _____ A black man overcomes hardship to care for his people.

10. _____ Jerry and Rachel must find their stolen puppy.

11. _____ Cusi must go on a journey to find a family.

continued on next page

NEWBERY MEDAL WINNERS 1943–63 (continued)

Write the letter of each title before the matching description.

A. Adam of the Road

B. Secret of the Andes

C. Johnny Tremain

D. And Now Miguel

E. Rabbit Hill

F. Wheel on the School

G. Strawberry Girl

H. Carry On Mr. Bowditch

I. Miss Hickory

J. Miracles on Maple Hill

K. Twenty-One Balloons

L. Rifles for Watie

M. King of the Wind

N. Witch of Blackbird Pond

O. Door in the Wall

P. Onion John

Q. Amos Fortune: Free Man

R. Island of the Blue Dolphins

S. Ginger Pye

T. Bronze Bow

U. Wrinkle in Time

12. _____ A boy longs to take the sheep to the mountains with the men.

13. _____ Children wonder why the storks won't settle in their village.

14. _____ Nat learns about ships and how to become a successful navigator.

15. _____ Marly hopes for a miracle to cure her sick father.

16. _____ A young boy leaves home to join the Union Army.

17. _____ An odd man who lives in a hut shares his strange beliefs with Andy.

18. _____ An Indian girl must survive alone on an island.

19. _____ A young boy in ancient Rome wants to avenge the death of his parents.

20. _____ Meg must fight an evil force to free her father from bondage.

21. _____ In 1687 Kit, a free spirit, makes friends with a woman suspected of being a witch.

Key: 1. A 2. C 3. E 4. G 5. I 6. K 7. M 8. O 9. Q 10. S 11. B 12. D 13. F 14. H 15. J 16. L 17. P 18. R 19. T 20. U 21. N

NEWBERY MEDAL WINNERS 1964–84

Complete each title below. Find and circle the missing words in the word search.

e	h	b	k	p	a	w	a	s	n
s	w	a	e	m	a	g	l	r	s
k	o	e	b	h	y	r	c	n	a
j	l	n	s	s	i	h	e	l	s
r	v	n	g	g	f	l	m	j	w
t	e	r	a	b	i	t	h	i	a
h	s	l	o	w	l	y	a	k	n
b	y	l	o	v	e	d	i	c	s
r	a	u	a	a	s	n	i	n	i
d	d	b	n	a	g	n	i	k	n

1. It's Like This _____
2. The High _____
3. Shadow of a _____
4. Roll of Thunder, Hear My ____
5. Juan de _____
6. Bridge to _____
7. Westing _____
8. Up A Road _____
9. A Gathering of _____

10. Mixed Up _____
11. Jacob I Have _____
12. The Grey _____
13. Visit to William Blake's _____
14. Summer of the _____
15. Dicey's _____
16. Mrs. Frisby and the Rats of ____
17. Dear Mr. _____
18. Julie of the _____

Key: 1. Cat 2. King 3. Bull 4. Cry 5. Pareja 6. Terabithia 7. Game
8. Slowly 9. Days 10. Files 11. Loved 12. King 13. Inn 14. Swans
15. Song 16. NIMH 17. Henshaw 18. Wolves

NEWBERY MEDAL WINNERS 1964–84

Write the letter of each title before the matching description.

A. It's Like This Cat
B. The High King
C. Shadow of a Bull
D. Roll of Thunder, Hear My Cry
E. I, Juan de Pareja
F. Bridge to Terabithia
G. Westing Game
H. Up A Road Slowly
I. A Gathering of Days
J. Mixed Up Files
U. Slave Dancer

K. Sounder
L. Jacob I Have Loved
M. The Grey King
N. Visit to William Blake's Inn
O. Summer of the Swans
P. Dicey's Song
Q. Mrs. Frisby and the Rats of NIMH
R. Dear Mr. Henshaw
S. Julie of the Wolves
T. M.C. Higgins the Great

1. _____ A young boy struggles to get along with his father.

2. _____ A boy searches for his father who is in a prison camp.

3. _____ A mouse appeals to rats to save her son.

4. _____ An assistant pig-keeper marches against evil forces with an army.

5. _____ A young girl survives on the Alaskan tundra with the help of wolves.

6. _____ Sarah forgets her troubles while searching for her retarded brother.

7. _____ Jesse is kidnapped and taken aboard a ship bound for Africa.

8. _____ Although forbidden to do so a slave teaches himself to paint.

9. _____ A mixed-up Julie goes to live with her aunt after her mother's death.

10. _____ Two children run away from home and hide out in a museum.

11. _____ A boy must save his family's home on grandmother Sarah's mountain.

12. _____ Will must awaken King Arthur's knights to battle the forces of Darkness.

continued on the next page

From *Books Every Child Should Know: The Literature Quiz Book* by Nancy Polette. Westport, CT: Libraries Unlimited. Copyright © 2006.

NEWBERY MEDAL WINNERS 1964–84 (continued)

Write the letter of each title before the matching description.

A. It's Like This Cat

B. The High King

C. Shadow of a Bull

D. Roll of Thunder, Hear My Cry

E. I, Juan de Pareja

F. Bridge to Terabithia

G. Westing Game

H. Up A Road Slowly

I. A Gathering of Days

J. Mixed Up Files

U. Slave Dancer

K. Sounder

L. Jacob I Have Loved

M. The Grey King

N. Visit to William Blake's Inn

O. Summer of the Swans

P. Dicey's Song

Q. Mrs. Frisby and the Rats of NIMH

R. Dear Mr. Henshaw

S. Julie of the Wolves

T. M.C. Higgins the Great

13. _____ Cassie stands up for her beliefs despite danger.

14. _____ A multimillionaire leaves a will instructing sixteen heirs to play a game in order to receive an inheritance.

15. _____ Should Catherine aid a runaway slave even though it is against the law?

16. _____ Louise feels she is a misfit and can't compete with her older sister.

17. _____ At this inn, angels shake featherbeds while Rabbit shows guests to their rooms.

18. _____ Unhappy Leigh writes all of his thoughts to his favorite author.

19. _____ A boy loses his best friend, who had created a magical kingdom for him.

20. _____ A boy is called a coward when he refuses to follow in his father's footsteps.

21. _____ Dicey and her siblings are sent to live with a grandmother whom they have never met.

Key: 1. A 2. K 3. Q 4. B 5. S 6. O 7. U 8. E 9. H 10. J 11. T 12. M
13. D 14. G 15. I 16. L 17. N 18. R 19. F 20. C 21. P

From *Books Every Child Should Know: The Literature Quiz Book* by Nancy Polette. Westport, CT: Libraries Unlimited. Copyright © 2006.

NEWBERY MEDAL WINNERS 1985–2005

Complete each title below. Find and circle the missing words in the word search.

c	g	i	v	e	r	w	a	a	a
r	r	a	b	c	m	o	o	n	s
y	m	o	s	i	r	i	p	k	a
r	y	a	w	t	a	l	l	i	t
r	d	u	g	n	a	p	e	r	u
t	d	l	e	e	d	r	u	a	r
x	u	a	e	r	e	p	s	e	d
s	b	i	a	p	s	a	d	a	a
y	n	h	p	p	i	n	t	a	y
t	s	u	d	a	o	w	a	a	a
t	y	a	u	y	n	p	m	i	w

1. Hero and the _____
2. View from _____
3. Sarah Plain and _____
4. Out of the _____
5. The Whipping _____
6. Bud, Not _____
7. Joyful _____
8. A Year Down _____
9. Number the _____

10. A Single _____
11. Maniac _____
12. Crispen: Cross of _____
13. Missing _____
14. Kira _____
15. The _____
16. Tale of _____
17. Walk Two _____
18. The Midwife's _____

Key: 1. Crown 2. Saturday 3. Tall 4. Dust 5. Boy 6. Buddy 7. Noise 8. Under 9. Stars 10. Shard 11. Magee 12. Lead 13. May 14. Kira 15. Giver 16. Despereaux 17. Moons 18. Apprentice

From Books Every Child Should Know: The Literature Quiz Book by Nancy Polette. Westport, CT: Libraries Unlimited. Copyright © 2006.

NEWBERY MEDAL WINNERS 1985–2005

Write the letter of each title before the matching description.

A. Hero and the Crown
B. View from Saturday
C. Sarah Plain and Tall
D. Out of the Dust
E. The Whipping Boy
F. Bud, Not Buddy
G. Lincoln: A Photobiography
H. Joyful Noise
 I. A Year Down Yonder
J. Number the Stars
K. The Midwife's Apprentice

L. A Single Shard
M. Maniac Magee
N. Crispen: Cross of Lead
O. Missing May
P. Kira Kira
Q. Holes
R. The Giver
S. Tale of Despereaux
T. Walk Two Moons
U. Shiloh

1. _____ Her battle with a dragon nearly kills young Aerin.

2. _____ Papa places an ad for a wife in a newspaper.

3. _____ Jemmy has to put up with thieves, kidnappers, and a spoiled prince.

4. _____ This book honors a great president.

5. _____ Read about grasshoppers, book lice, and honeybees.

6. _____ Annemarie's family helps her Jewish friend, Ellen, escape from the Nazis.

7. _____ A boy lives in two worlds, on the east and the west side of town.

8. _____ Marty rescues a dog from a mean owner, but his family is too poor to feed it.

9. _____ Summer goes to live with her uncle and aunt, and meets strange characters.

10. _____ Jonas lives in a world without color, feelings, or emotions.

11. _____ Sal takes a long trip with her grandparents in search of her mother.

continued on next page

NEWBERY MEDAL WINNERS 1985–2005 (continued)

Write the letter of each title before the matching description.

A. Hero and the Crown

B. View from Saturday

C. Sarah Plain and Tall

D. Out of the Dust

E. The Whipping Boy

F. Bud, Not Buddy

G. Lincoln: A Photobiography

H. Joyful Noise

I. A Year Down Yonder

J. Number the Stars

K. The Midwife's Apprentice

L. A Single Shard

M. Maniac Magee

N. Crispen: Cross of Lead

O. Missing May

P. Kira Kira

Q. Holes

R. The Giver

S. Tale of Despereaux

T. Walk Two Moons

U. Shiloh

12. _____ Beetle is found in a dung heap by a cranky woman who works her hard and gives her little food.

13. _____ A sixth grade class wins an Academic Bowl, but mystery surrounds how the team members were chosen.

14. _____ Billie Jo is angry at the hard life she must live in the Dust Bowl of the '30s.

15. _____ Stanley ends up at a camp for bad boys for a crime he did not commit.

16. _____ A young boy hitchhikes to Michigan in search of his father,

17. _____ Mary Alice is sent to live with her feisty grandmother.

18. _____ Tree-ear lives under a bridge but longs to become a master potter.

19. _____ A boy in fourteenth-century England meets a juggler who has a dangerous secret.

20. _____ A small mouse falls in love with a princess and wants to be her hero.

21. _____ A hard-working Japanese family moves to Georgia with hope for a better life.

Key: 1. A 2. C 3. E 4. G 5. H 6. J 7. M 8. U 9. O 10. R 11. T 12. K 13. B 14. D 15. Q 16. F 17. I 18. L 19. N 20. S 21. P

NEWBERY MEDAL AND HONOR BOOKS
Animal Story Scavenger Hunt

Visit the library shelves. Find the topic for each Dewey number. Write each topic on the line after its number. Match the book descriptions with the titles by writing the number of the title after each description.

Titles

1. Charlotte's Web
2. The Cricket in Times Square
3. Doctor DeSoto
4. Ginger Pye
5. Julie of the Wolves
6. King of the Wind
7. Mr. Popper's Penguins
8. Mrs. Frisby and the Rats of NIMH
9. Rabbit Hill
10. Shiloh
11. Smoky the Cowhorse
12. Tale of Despereaux
13. Voyages of Dr. Doolittle

A. A tiny, large-eared **636.08** _____ who falls in love with a princess is banished by his own father to the foul, rat-filled **728.8** _____ dungeon.

_____

B. A boy finds a **636.7** _____ and tries to hide it from his family and the owner, a mean man who mistreats animals.

_____

C. A man tries to learn the language of **597** _____ with the help of Jip. the **636.7** _____ and Deb-dab the **598** _____.

_____

D. A **636.1** _____ of the wild **978** _____ is stolen by rustlers to appear on the rodeo circuit until broken and destined for the slaughter house.

_____

E. A man receives a **598** _____ from **998** _____ and has trouble finding a place to keep it.

_____

F. Georgie, the **636.088** _____ is injured by a **629.222** _____ but is given tender care by a family who loves animals.

_____

continued on next page

NEWBERY MEDAL AND HONOR BOOKS

Animal Story Scavenger Hunt (continued)

G. In a stable in **909** _____ a mute boy falls in love with a **636.1** _____ that has a tiny white mark on its off hind heel, an emblem of swiftness.

_____

H. Papa is a famous **598** _____ expert. Jerry wants to be a **549** _____ man. Someone has stolen Rachel s very smart little **636.7** _____ and the whole family is determined never to give up until they find her.

_____

I. A **595.7** _____ travels to **973.4** _____ and lives in Mario's newsstand and discovers that he can imitate perfectly any **784.19** _____ he hears.

_____

J. Her youngest son is very ill and his mother cannot move him before the plow destroys her underground **630.1** _____ home. She seeks help from rats with super **153** _____ who had escaped from a **362.1** _____ laboratory.

_____

K. A young **970.004** _____ girl becomes lost on the Alaskan **574.5** _____ and survives when she is adopted by **599.74** _____. She learns their language and earns their trust.

_____

L. A mouse **617.6** _____ finds a way to make sure he is not eaten by a **599.74** _____ who wants to be his patient.

_____

M. Charlotte, the **595.4** _____ who lives on a **630.1** _____finds a unique way to save Wilbur the pig from being sent to the butcher.

_____

Key: A) Tale of Despereaux/mouse/castle B) Shiloh/dog C) Voyages of Dr. Doolittle/fish/dog/duck or birds D) Smoky the Cowhorse/horse/West E) Mr. Popper's Penguins/penguin or bird/Antarctica F) Rabbit Hill/rabbit/car G) King of the Wind/Arabia/horse H) Ginger Pye/bird/rock/dog, I) The Cricket in Times Square/cricket or insect/New York/music J) Mrs. Frisby and the Rats of NIMH/farm/intelligent/hospital K) Julie of the Wolves /Inuit/tundra/wolves L) Doctor DeSoto/dentist/fox M) Charlotte's Web/spider/farm

From *Books Every Child Should Know: The Literature Quiz Book* by Nancy Polette. Westport, CT: Libraries Unlimited. Copyright © 2006.

NEWBERY MEDAL AND HONOR BOOKS
Historical Fiction Time Periods

A. Middle Ages   E. Civil War
B. Colonial Period   F. Late 1800s
C. Revolutionary War   G. Early 1900s
D. Early 1800s   H. World War II

I. On the line before each title write the letter corresponding to the time period of the story.

1. _____ Bud, Not Buddy   9. _____ Rifles for Watie
2. _____ Door In the Wall   10. _____ Sarah Plain and Tall
3. _____ A Gathering of Days   11. _____ Sign of the Beaver
4. _____ Johnny Tremain   12. _____ Sing Down the Moon
5. _____ Matchlock Gun   13. _____ Slave Dancer
6. _____ Midwife's Apprentice   14. _____ Sounder
7. _____ Number the Stars   15. _____ Witch of Blackbird Pond
8. _____ Out of the Dust   16. _____ Year Down Yonder

II. Write the number of each title by its description.

A. _____ Ten-year-old Edward uses an old gun to protect his family from a raid.
B. _____ A young boy searches for his father, imprisoned for stealing food.
C. _____ A girl writes in her journal of her father's remarriage.
D. _____ Children spend a summer with their eccentric grandmother.
E. _____ Buddy seeks his father, believing him to be a famous musician.
F. _____ Robin dreams of being a knight but cannot walk.
G. _____ A lively girl from Barbados makes friends with one believed to be a witch.
H. _____ Life in the Depression is hard when a family loses its mother.
I. _____ Johnny gives up his dream of being a silversmith after he burns his hand.
J. _____ Jessie plays his fife on a slave ship.
K. _____ A woman is jealous of the young orphan girl who is her servant.
L. _____ A Native American tribe is forced on a long march to a desolate land.
M. _____ A boy joins the Union Army after bushwhackers torment his family.
N. _____ After his gun is stolen, a boy survives with the help of a young brave.
O. _____ Papa places an ad for a wife in a newspaper.
P. _____ Anne Marie learns firsthand about the cruelties of war.

Key: I. 1. G 2. A 3. D 4. C 5. B 6. A 7. H 8. G 9. F 10. F 11. B
12. E 13. D 14. F 15. B 16. G
II. A. 5 B. 14 C. 3 D. 16 E. 1 F. 2 G. 15 H. 8 I. 4 J. 13 K. 6
L. 12 M. 9 N. 11 O. 10 P. 7

From *Books Every Child Should Know: The Literature Quiz Book* by Nancy Polette. Westport, CT: Libraries Unlimited. Copyright © 2006.

NEWBERY MEDAL AND HONOR BOOKS

Tales From Other Lands

Match each title with the country or region in which the story takes place. Some countries are used more than once.

1. _____ The Dark Frigate   A. China

2. _____ Shen of the Sea   B. Denmark

3. _____ Tales from Silver Lands   C. England

4. _____ Trumpeter of Krakow   D. Hungary

5. _____ The White Stag   E. Holland

6. _____ Call It Courage   F. Poland

7. _____ Door in the Wall   G. Polynesia

8. _____ Wheel on the School   H. South America

9. _____ Shadow of a Bull   I. Spain

10. _____ I, Juan de Pareja

11. _____ Number the Stars

Key: 1. C 2. A 3. H 4. F 5. D 6. G 7. C 8. E 9. I 10. I 11. B

NEWBERY TITLE GAME

Decode these titles by replacing the words in each with synonyms.

EXAMPLE:

1. A Narrative Account of Homo Sapiens
   The Story of Mankind
   _____

2. The Ocean Travels of a Physician of Little Expenditure of Energy
   _____

3. A Product of Conflagration: the Bovine Steed
   _____

4. Joyful Appendage Attached to the Head
   _____

5. The Feline Ascending to the Abode of the Almighty
   _____

6. An Elevated Mass Lacking One Part Hydrogen and Two Parts Oxygen
   _____

7. A Metal Object for a Member of the Hand in the Warmest Season of the Year
   _____

8. Designate It Intrepidness
   _____

9. A Small Natural Elevation with Burrowing Rodents
   _____

10. Monarch of Air in Motion
    _____

11. An Entrance within a Structure Enclosing a Space
    _____

12. A Circular Frame Attached to an Institution of Learning
    _____

13. A Furrow of Indefinite Duration
    _____

continued on next page

NEWBERY TITLE GAME (continued)

14. Ascending a Public Passage Tediously

15. Monarch of Herculean Elevation

16. Young Male Undergoing Corporal Punishment

17. Estatic Clamor

18. Calculate the Nightly Luminaries

19. The Bountiful One

20. Promenade Duplicate Lunas

21. Ascending from Finite Particles of Earth

22. Excavations

23. One Fragment of an Earthen Vessel

Key: 2. Voyages of Dr. Doolittle 3. Smoky the Cowhorse 4. Gay Neck
5. Cat Who Went to Heaven 6. Waterless Mountain 7. Thimble
Summer 8. Call It Courage 9. Rabbit Hill 10. King of the Wind
11. Door in the Wall 12. Wheel on the School 13. Wrinkle in Time
14. Up a Road Slowly 15. High King 16. Whipping Boy 17. Joyful
Noise 18. Number the Stars 19. The Giver 20. Walk Two Moons
21. Out of the Dust 22. Holes 23. A Single Shard

From *Books Every Child Should Know: The Literature Quiz Book*
by Nancy Polette. Westport, CT: Libraries Unlimited. Copyright © 2006.

NEWBERY TITLE GAME: HONOR BOOKS

Decode these titles by replacing the words in each with synonyms.

EXAMPLE

1. Ten Hundred Thousands of Felines
   Millions of Cats
2. The Benevolent Employer
   _____
3. A Warbling Plant Possessing a Woody Trunk
   _____
4. An Extended Season Between Autumn and Spring
   _____
5. A Miniscule Metropolis upon Grassland
   _____
6. Garments Ten Times Ten
   _____
7. A Symbolic Device Adorning the Atmosphere
   _____
8. The Clandestine Estuary
   _____
9. Departed Inland Body of Standing Water
   _____
10. Related Members Beneath a Viaduct
    _____
11. A Hostelry of Great Trepidation
    _____
12. An Enclosure upon an Ascending Level
    _____
13. A Circle of Continuing Illumination
    _____

continued on next page

NEWBERY TITLE GAME: HONOR BOOKS (continued)

14. The Benefactor of Desires

15. A Feline with a Singular Organ of Sight

16. An Enclosed Space between Autumn and Spring

17. A Plethora of Veracity

18. Erratic Female

19. The Humongous Conflagration

20. One Who Meanders

continued on next page

NEWBERY TITLE GAME: HONOR BOOKS: KEY

1. *Millions of Cats* by Wanda Gag. New York, Coward McCann, 1929.

2. *The Good Master* by Kate Seredy. New York, Viking, 1936.

3. *The Singing Tree* by Kate Seredy. New York, Viking, 1939.

4. *The Long Winter* by Laura Ingalls Wilder. New York, Harper & Row, 1941.

5. *Little Town on the Prairie* by Laura Ingalls Wilder. New York, Harper & Row, 1942.

6. *The Hundred Dresses* by Eleanor Estes. New York, Harcourt, 1955.

7. *Banner in the Sky* by James Ramsey Ullman. New York, Lippincott, 1955.

8. *The Secret River* by Marjorie Kinan Rawlings. New York, Scribners, 1952.

9. *Gone-Away Lake* by Elizabeth Enright. New York, Harcourt, 1958.

10. *Family under the Bridge* by Natalie Carlson. New York, Harper & Row, 1959.

11. *Fearsome Inn* by Isaac Bashevis Singer. New York, Scribners, 1989.

12. *The Upstairs Room* by Johanna Reiss. New York, Crowell, 1973.

13. *Ring of Endless Light* by Madeleine L'Engle. New York, Farrar, 1981.

14. *The Wish Giver* by Bill Brittain. New York, HarperCollins, 1984.

15. *One-Eyed Cat* by Paula Fox. New York, Bradbury, 1985.

16. *The Winter Room* by Gary Paulsen. New York, Orchard, 1990.

17. *Nothing But the Truth* by Avi. New York, Orchard, 1992.

18. *Crazy Lady* by Jane Leslie Conly. New York, HarperCollins, 1994.

19. *The Great Fire* by Jim Murphy. New York, Scholastic, 1996.

20. *The Wanderer* by Sharon Creech. New York, HarperColllins, 2001.

NEWBERY MEDAL AND HONOR BOOKS

Realistic Fiction

Underline the titles of Newbery Award–winning books of realistic fiction that are hidden in the story.

Here is the strange story of a boy named Bud, not Buddy. I found the tale in the mixed-up files of Mrs. Basil E. Frankweiler. It seems that Bud wanted to show his girlfriend, Ginger Pye, a strange sight, so they went for a walk. Two moons were in the sky. Ginger could not believe her eyes.

Bud shouted, "What a view! From Saturday until today those moons haven't moved!"

Ginger replied, "What miracles! On Maple Hill where I live there is only one moon. Oh, dear! Mr. Henshaw, the science teacher, must see this. Let s go find him."

Bud wanted to share his discovery with others, so he called his friends John, Maniac Magee, who always had holes in his jeans, and M.C. Higgins. "The great sight is up in the sky," he told them.

After a time the boys got hungry so Ginger opened a lunch box. "Have a pickled onion, John," she offered. "Only the napkins are missing. May is a wonderful month for eating onions under two moons."

Just then they heard a roll of thunder. "Hear my cry," Bud shouted. "We need to get home before it storms."

Sad to say, later that night when the storms had cleared, the two moons were gone, never to be seen again.

Key: Bud, Not Buddy; Ginger Pye, Miracles on Maple Hill, Onion John, From the Mixed Up Files of Mrs. Basil E. Frankweiler, M.C. Higgins the Great; Roll of Thunder, Hear My Cry; Dear Mr. Henshaw, Maniac Magee, Missing May, Walk Two Moons, A View from Saturday, Holes

---

From *Books Every Child Should Know: The Literature Quiz Book*
by Nancy Polette. Westport, CT: Libraries Unlimited. Copyright © 2006.

NEWBERY AWARD–WINNING AUTHOR: AVI

Underline titles of books by Avi hidden in this story.

Things that sometimes happen on Ereth's birthday are very strange. It takes place on Christmas each year. Last year Ereth invited Crispen. The cross of lead he brought was a strange birthday present.

This year, Poppy and Rye had been grounded and had to escape from home to attend Ereth's party. A windcatcher, a wolf rider, and a midnight magic show by Perloo the bold were to be the entertainment. Poppy went to the barn to find her dog, Ragweed. The dog was missing. A party would not be a party without that good dog.

About that time Poppy's friend Abigail drove up. Poppy told her that Ragweed was missing. "Who was that masked man anyway that I saw behind your barn?" Abigail asked.

"Maybe it was a dognapper," Poppy cried. "Let's go look on Smuggler's Island." Abigail takes the wheel. She broke speed limits. "Slow down," Poppy cried.

"Don't you know there's a war on?" Abigail yelled. "We are at war with a dognapper." She sped past Lord Kirkle's. "Money is what they want, but we are going to meet them on their own fighting ground!" she continued.

She brought the car to a screeching halt. There, on their way to the party, were Romeo and Juliet together. Romeo was carrying a blue heron he planned to give Ereth as a present. Juliet had Ragweed on a leash. "We found Ragweed chasing a rat," they said.

Poppy laughed. "Let's go to Ereth's party. My strange present to her will be the rat. But we'll have to keep it a secret. School will never be the same after Christmas vacation when Ereth shows up with her new pet."

The party was a great success and Ereth loved all of her presents, especially the Christmas rat!

NEWBERY AWARD–WINNING AUTHOR: BETSY BYARS

Underline titles of books by Betsy Byars hidden in this story.

Cracker Jackson was a computer nut. Everyone took their problems to him. His most frequent customer was Bingo Brown. The burning questions of Bingo Brown kept Cracker busy at the computer for hours. Another customer was the keeper of the doves at the zoo. When the birds flew away, Cracker was asked to find them.

When the Golly sisters' cat pulled another of its disappearing acts, they went to see Cracker. After a three day absence they were afraid Mud Blossom might be in big trouble. River currents were strong this year and the cat might have gotten too close to the water. Cracker sent out a computer SOS. It read, "Wanted: Mud Blossom!" A reply came from a computer geek named McMummy. It said that if the Golly sisters go west two blocks they will find their cat. Hooray for the Golly sisters! They found Mud Blossom had taken up residence with an author named Jones. He was writing a book about the animal, the vegetable, and John D. Jones.

One problem Cracker could not solve with his computer was his little brother, Ant. Cracker often said, "My brother, Ant, just won't grow up. One day Ant plays bear. He roars at everyone. The next day he's swinging from trees hollering, "Me, Tarzan!"

Ant was like a tornado everywhere he went. When he sprayed the water hose on Cracker's girlfriend, Cybil, war was declared. Cracker's friend, Tarot, sent letters to everyone in town. The letters read. Tarot says beware! If you see Ant, go hide in the nearest dark stairs until he passes by! Unfortunately, Tarot forgot to put the zip codes on the letters and they ended up in the dead letter office.

If Cracker ever figures out a way to solve his little brother's problems on the computer, he will be the first to let everyone who has a little brother know.

NEWBERY AWARD–WINNING AUTHOR: SHARON CREECH

Underline titles of books by Sharon Creech hidden in this story.

Ruby Holler was a wanderer. She could not stay in one place more than a few days. Although some people thought this was absolutely normal, chaos happened wherever she went. When she passed by flowers, they lost their bloomability. A fine, fine school she attended for three days had its roof fall in. The principal told her in no uncertain terms to take a walk!

Two moons passed before Ruby found a new place to stay. It was a haunted house. No one else wanted to live there. Pleasing the ghost dog who haunted the house was impossible. It howled night and day. Ruby decided to love that dog and as soon as she did, the howling ceased. She named the dog Redbird and loved chasing Redbird up and down the rickety stairs. The dog loved the game, too.

One day Ruby and the ghost dog went fishing. In the air she saw a small plane. For a moment she thought about wandering again, but then she looked at Redbird. He was the first real friend she had ever had so, she decided to spend the rest of her days in the haunted house.

NEWBERY AWARD–WINNING AUTHOR: PAULA FOX

Underline titles of books by Paula Fox hidden in this story.

Amzat and his brothers were very poor. Of money they had very little. Swineherd pay was not enough to put food on the table. One brother tried to make money by selling peeks at his one-eyed cat. Another served as a guide to see the wild monkeys on Monkey Island. Still, they were very poor. Amzat had only two possessions to call his own, a pipe and an eagle kite.

One day the brothers saw an ad for a slave dancer. Amzat played his pipe so well that now and then listeners tossed him a penny or two. His brothers decided he could make more money if he played for slaves to dance. The ad said to report to the village by the sea. Amzat did and got the job. He played so beautifully that the guards went to sleep. Amzat opened the gates and the slaves ran as if carried by the western wind.

Amzat was not a bit sorry when he lost his job. He still had his pipe and his eagle kite and was a free man, as every man should be.

NEWBERY AWARD–WINNING AUTHOR: JEAN CRAIGHEAD GEORGE

Underline titles of books by Jean Craighead George hidden in this story.

Julie was the first woman conservation agent in the country. She took the job very seriously. At night she took Vulpes the red fox home with her. Visitors who wanted to clean up at Julie's house find there's an owl in the shower. When robbers asked her for money, she told them "There's a tarantula in my purse." They ran away.

Julie loved animals and would do anything to help them. Once when searching for the missing gator of Gumbo Limbo, she had to climb a waterfall in the Everglades. The first Thanksgiving that Julie had the job, she celebrated with the animals by making them acorn pancakes, dandelion salad, and other wild recipes. Every moon of the gray wolves, Julie would go on the far side of the mountain to visit her furry friends. Her nickname became Julie of the wolves.

One day in the woods Julie found an injured deer. She named the deer Rebecca and spoke to it as if it were a person. "Dear Rebecca, winter is here," she said. "Copper Creek runs right by my cabin and a mother deer comes there to drink every day. I call her the dipper of Copper Creek. If she sees you perhaps she will adopt you."

That is exactly what happened, and to this very day Julie continues to care for her animal friends.

NEWBERY AWARD–WINNING AUTHOR: KAREN HESSE

Underline titles of books by Karen Hesse hidden in this story.

Sable lives in the United States. Her pen pal, Rifka, lives in Poland. Letters from Rifka are always a treat. Rifka has a great sense of humor. In one letter she told about her friend, Lester. His dog liked to chase rats until one day it got nipped on the nose. The dog spent as much time at Rifka's house as it did at Lester's.

In another letter Rifka told about a voyage she took on the Mediteranian Sea. She sailed on a ship named the *Phoenix.* It was a wonderful trip except for strange sounds coming from the hold. The passengers thought it might be a ghost. The captain assured everyone that it was only the music of dolphins, but no one believed him.

One evening the sounds were louder than usual. Rifka decided to investigate. She climbed down into the hold of the *Phoenix.* Rising out of the dust was Lester's dog! The stowaway had followed her on to the ship. Rifka had heard that on this ship stowaways are usually thrown overboard. It must have been a time of angels because Rifka was allowed to keep the dog in her cabin until the ship docked.

Yes! Letters from Rifka were always fun to read!

NEWBERY AWARD–WINNING AUTHOR: LOIS LOWRY

Underline titles of books by Lois Lowry hidden in this story.

Anastasia Krupnik has four best friends, Caroline, Zooman Sam, J.P., and Rabble Starkey. Anastasia absolutely loved her dog, Blue. That was why she was so upset when Blue disappeared. Usually Anastasia has the answers but not this time. She sent an email to her friends. She said, "Come meet with Anastasia at this address on Autumn Street. It will be an important gathering. Blue has disappeared."

Caroline was the first to arrive. The one hundreth thing about Caroline is that she is full of questions and advice. "Did the dog run all about? Sam may have seen him. Did you ask? Did you tell the dog to stay? I know you are upset, Anastasia. Ask your analyst for some pills to calm you down. We should check every house number? The stars will be out before we are done. What should we do first? It's your move."

J.P. was next to arrive. He was late because he had to look after his little brother, Terrific. Taking care of Terrific was no easy job. He asked his sister to switch around jobs with him so that he could help look for Blue. The day was getting hotter when Rabble showed up. It was a summer to die of the heat, but the children didn't notice. They had to find Blue. Rabble asked Anastasia again where she had last seen Blue.

"Next door at Miss Perkins," Anastasia replied. "Blue knows she is a giver of treats but he's not there now."

Just then Sam heard a noise under the porch. He crawled under and out he came with Blue. The dog had crawled under the porch to keep cool.

"Attaboy, Sam!" the friends cried. "You found Blue!" The friends all started home. Before Sam left, Anastasia gave him a thank you and a big kiss. "See you around, Sam," she grinned.

She never saw Sam again.

NEWBERY AWARD–WINNING AUTHOR:
PATRICIA MACLACHLAN

Underline the titles of books by Patricia MacLachlan hidden in this story.

Arthur, Caleb, Cassie, and Sarah were positive that Minna Pratt was a witch. In the town of Skylark there were lots of facts and fictions of Minna Pratt. It was hard to tell which was which. One day Cassie Binegar asked her grandpa about Minna.

"What you know first," Grandpa said, "is that she lives alone. Once she had three names, Minna Mary Pratt, but folks just call her Minna now. She cured Mrs. Jacob's baby of the croup. She helped Arthur. For the very first time he talked without stuttering. She told Sarah, plain and tall, that she would get seven kisses in a row and that's just what happened. Since I've been taking her tonic I've never had a sick day."

Cassie told her friends what Grandpa had said. Through Grandpa's eyes, Minna Pratt was a good woman who helped everyone who asked. Because of Minna, Skylark was the best place to live of all the places on the planet.

"To love your neighbor is a good thing," the children decided. Now when they go past Minna's house they wave and say hello. Minna always waves back.

From *Books Every Child Should Know: The Literature Quiz Book*
by Nancy Polette. Westport, CT: Libraries Unlimited. Copyright © 2006.

NEWBERY AWARD–WINNING AUTHOR: SCOTT O'DELL

Underline titles of books by Scott O'Dell in hidden in this story.

All night long Sarah Bishop stared at the black star. Bright dawn made the star disappear, but Sarah was worried. Sarah's parents were missionaries. Their home was on the Island of the Blue Dolphins. Sarah had heard many rumblings of late. The natives were sure that a great disaster was coming. They had many superstitions. If anyone dared to sing, down the moon would come and crush the island. If a black pearl is brought up by a diver, they must leave the island, taking their canoes on streams to the river, river to the sea, never to return.

Sarah's parents tried to convince the natives that these things were not true. The natives replied that thunder rolling in the mountains means the serpent never sleeps and the serpent is a symbol of bad luck.

One night the Chief had a dream. In his dream a dove flew down from the sky. The dove spoke to him. "Listen to my name. Is not Angelica another name for angel? I am the angel of your island. No disaster will befall you. Listen to the missionaries. They are your friends."

The next morning when the chief awoke, there by his sleeping mat was the feather of a dove. Later that morning the chief led the entire island to the home of the missionaries. "You are good people," he said. "We will listen to your stories." Sarah smiled. There would be no disaster on this island.

NEWBERY AWARD–WINNING AUTHOR: KATHERINE PATERSON

Underline titles of books by Katherine Paterson hidden in this story.

Jimmy Jo was a preacher's boy. His father was the Reverend Jacob Glass. Jimmy Jo couldn't wait to visit his brother, Marvin. One too many times Marvin had been in trouble. He was in prison near a town called Terabithia. Christmas was coming. Jimmy Jo wanted to take Marvin a present. He wanted it to be Marvin's best Christmas present ever. He wrote Marvin a letter and asked what he wanted for Christmas. Marvin wrote that if Jimmy Jo sang for him that would be better than any present. Jimmy Jo had a wonderful voice.

Jimmy Jo had two sisters, Lyddie and Zia. People called Zia a flip-flop girl because she was always changing her mind. One day she said she would go with the family to visit Marvin on Christmas. The next day she said staying home would be great. Gilly Hopkins, her friend, would keep her company.

Jimmy Jo, Lyddie and their parents began their trip early in the morning. They stopped at King's store. At King's, equal muffins were bought for Marvin, half chocolate and half cranberry.

As they were leaving, Jimmy Jo almost stepped on Mr. King's dog, Jip. His story was almost as sad as Marvin's. A farmer had taken a bunch of stray dogs into his field with his shotgun. Of the dogs who tried to escape, Jip was the only one who made it. Now he had a good life with Mr. King.

The family was almost to the prison when they hit a roadblock. The bridge to Terabithia was out and they would have to detour on a rough road through the woods. When the prison finally came in sight, Jimmy Jo's mother spoke to his father.

"Jacob, have I loved all my children equally? I think so but when we enter the prison gates I do think about what a trial Marvin has been to us. He just keeps doing the same stuff. As stars are in the sky I have tried my best to be a good mother."

Jimmy Jo's father gave his mother a hug. "You have been a fine mother," he said. "I do believe Marvin has learned the error of his ways. When he is released in three months it will be the last he will ever see of a prison. Now let's go and help him have a merry Christmas. Come sing, Jimmy Jo. Make it merry for everyone."

And he did!

NEWBERY AWARD–WINNING AUTHOR: ZILPHA KEATLEY SNYDER

Underline titles of books by Zilpha Keatley Snyder hidden in this story.

There was great excitement in the Land of Egypt. Game day was coming! Gib was a pickpocket. Gib was also a gypsy. Game day was his most profitable day of the year. There were many pockets to pick. People did not pay attention to their pockets when they were watching the games.

Gib lived in a gypsy camp named the Witches of Worm. The gypsies thought that the name might scare people off. The artist in the camp was Libby. On Wednesday she had painted a headless cupid on the gate. She was sure that would keep people away. Gypsies did not welcome trespassers.

The day of the games was bright and clear. The first game was the cat race. Libby had entered her cat. Running against Libby's cat was the Pharaoh's cat.The Pharaoh's cat always won. The signal was given and the cats streaked forward like runaways being chased by dogs. In the meantime, Gib reached out to pick the pocket of a man in a gray suit. He felt nothing but air. He tried again. Again he felt nothing but air. When the man turned around Gib saw the man had no face. Gib and the gray ghost stared at each other for a long moment. Then the gray ghost vanished into thin air.

Libby's cat came in second in the race. The Pharaoh's cat won again. When the games were over Gib rides home with Libby vowing never to pick a pocket again.

NEWBERY AWARD–WINNING AUTHOR: JERRY SPINELLI

Underline titles of books by Jerry Spinelli hidden in this story.

Maniac Magee was the yo-yo champion of Shuster School. Tooter Pepperday was the yo-yo champion of Wringer School. The big yo-yo contest between the two schools was ready to begin.

Who would be the winner?

Unknown to Maniac, the fourth grade rats of Wringer School, led by a rat named Stargirl, had tied knots in Maniac's yo-yo string. Maniac lost the contest. "There were knots in my yo-yo string," he said. "It's enough to give anyone the blue ribbon blues."

Just then he saw Stargirl with a big smirk on her face. He knew who had tied the knots! He grabbed her and threw her to the ground. "There's a girl in my hammerlock," he yelled, "and I'm not going to let her up until she tells what she did."

Stargirl refused to talk. She got no help from the fourth grade rats. Maniac refused to let her up. Maniac's friend, Skeeter, pulled out his library card. It reminded him of a book he had read about water torture. He ran to the side of the school and turned on the hose. He sprayed Stargirl and every one of the fourth grade rats. He looked at the wet and dripping kids. "You should call yourselves the Bathwater Gang," he said.

Maniac let go of Stargirl when she confessed that she had tied the knots. The contest was repeated and Maniac won. "You need a crash course in yo-yo spinning," he told Tooter. "Come over to my house tomorrow and I'll teach you how to do it."

Today Maniac Magee and Tooter Pepperday are the yo-yo champions of the country. As a team they are unbeatable!

From *Books Every Child Should Know: The Literature Quiz Book*
by Nancy Polette. Westport, CT: Libraries Unlimited. Copyright © 2006.

NEWBERY AWARD–WINNING AUTHOR: MILDRED D. TAYLOR

Underline titles of books by Mildred D. Taylor hidden in this story.

Cadillac always wore a ring made of gold. Cadillac found the ring on a Mississippi bridge and called it his good luck ring. He knew it brought good luck because on the road to Memphis he found an old bicycle someone had abandoned. In no time he had that old bike fixed up like new. There is no greater friendship than that of a boy and his bike.

Cadillac loved nature. He would hop on his fixed-up bike every chance he got and head for the woods three miles out of town. He liked hearing the song of the trees when the wind whistled through them. He liked hearing the rustle of the little animals in the brush. Once he saw a sleek deer jump a fence right in front of him.

Early one evening Cadillac was alone in the woods when he heard a roll of thunder. "Hear my cry," a voice cried out. "Help, help, I am trapped in the well."

Cadillac raced in the direction of the voice. Sure enough he found an old abandoned well. Trapped at the bottom was a strange little man. Cadillac tossed the man a rope and pulled him out. The little man was dressed in a green suit and had pointed ears. "Thank you, kind sir," he said. "Now I must do something for you. I see you have lost your ring."

Cadillac looked at his hand. His good luck charm was gone! "Don't worry," the little man told Cadillac. He drew an imaginary circle on Cadillac's hand. "Don't wash your hand for one whole day," the little man said. "Let the circle be unbroken for twenty-four hours and good luck will be yours forever."

In the wink of an eye the little man disappeared. Cadillac did not wash his hand for one full day and he has had good luck ever since.

NEWBERY AUTHORS HIDDEN TITLES: KEY

Avi

Abigail Takes the Wheel. Harper, 1999.
Barn. Orchard, 1994.
Blue Heron. Macmillan, 1992.
Christmas Rat. Atheneum, 2000.
Crispin, The Cross of Lead. Hyperion, 2002
Don't You Know There's A War On? Hyperion, 2001.
Ereth's Birthday. Harper, 2000.
Escape from Home. Orchard, 1996.
Fighting Ground. Harper, 1984.
Good Dog. Atheneum, 2001.
Lord Kirkle's Money. Orchard, 1996.
Midnight Magic. Scholastic, 1999.
Nothing But the Truth. Orchard, 1991.
Perloo the Bold. Scholastic, 1998.
Poppy. Orchard, 1995.
Poppy and Rye. Avon, 1998.
Prairie School. Harper, 2001.
Ragweed. Harper, 1999.
Romeo and Juliet Together. Orchard, 1997
Secret School. Harcourt, 2001.
Smuggler's Island. Beech Tree, 1994.
Something Upstairs. Orchard, 1998.
Things That Sometimes Happen. Atheneum, 2002.
Who Was That Masked Man Anyway? Orchard, 1992.
Windcatcher. Bradbury, 1991.
Wolf Rider. Simon & Schuster, 1986.

Betsy Byars

The Animal, The Vegetable and John D. Jones. Doubleday, 1985.
Ant Plays Bear. Viking, 1997.
The Burning Questions of Bingo Brown. Viking, 1988.
Computer Nut. Viking, 1986.
Cracker Jackson. Viking, 1986.
Cybil War. Viking, 1990.
Dark Stairs. Viking, 1994.
Dead Letter. Viking, 1996
Death's Door. Viking, 1997.
Disappearing Acts. Viking, 1998.
Golly Sisters Go West. Harper, 1989.
Hooray for the Golly Sisters. Harper, 1992.
Keeper of the Doves. Viking, 2002.
McMummy. Viking, 1993.
Me, Tarzan. Harper, 2000.
My Brother, Ant. Viking, 1996.
Tarot Says Beware. Viking, 1995.

From *Books Every Child Should Know: The Literature Quiz Book*
by Nancy Polette. Westport, CT: Libraries Unlimited. Copyright © 2006.

Tornado. Harper, 1996.
Trouble River. Viking, 1989.
Wanted . . . Mud Blossom. Delacorte, 1991.

Sharon Creech

Absolutely Normal Chaos. Harper, 1995.
Bloomability. Harper, 1998.
Chasing Redbird. Harper, 1997.
Fine, Fine School. Harper, 2001.
Fishing in the Air. Harper, 2000.
Love That Dog. Harper, 2001.
Pleasing the Ghost. Harper, 1996.
Ruby Holler. Harper, 2002.
Walk Two Moons. Harper, 1994.
Wanderer. Harper, 2000.

Paula Fox

Amzat and His Brothers. Orchard, 1993.
Eagle Kite. Orchard, 1995.
Little Swineherd. Dutton, 1995.
Monkey Island. Orchard, 1991.
One-Eyed Cat. Bradbury, 1984.
Slave Dancer. Bradbury, 1973.
Village By the Sea. Orchard, 1988.
Western Wind. Orchard, 1993.

Jean Craighead George

Acorn Pancakes, Dandelion Salad and 38 Other Wild Recipies. Harper, 1995.
Dear Rebecca, Winter Is Here. Harper, 1993.
Dipper of Copper Creek. Dutton, 1996.
Everglades. Harper, 1995.
First Thanksgiving. Philomel, 1993.
Julie. Harper, 1994.
Julie of the Wolves. Harper, 1973.
Look to the North. Harper, 1997.
Missing 'Gator of Gumbo Limbo. Harper, 1992.
Moon of the Gray Wolves. Harper, 1991.
My Side of the Mountain. Dutton, 1988.
On the Far Side of the Mountain. Dutton, 1990.
One Day in the Woods. Harper, 1988.
Tarantula in My Purse. Harper, 1996.
There's An Owl in the Shower. Harper, 1995.
To Climb a Waterfall. Philomel, 1995.
Vulpes the Red Fox. Dutton, 1996.

Karen Hesse

Lester's Dog. Coward, 1996.
Letters from Rifka. Holt, 1992.

Music of Dolphins. Scholastic, 1996.
Out of the Dust. Scholastic, 1997.
Phoenix Rising. Holt, 1994.
Sable. Holt, 1994.
Stowaway. Simon & Schuster, 2000.
Time of Angels. Hyperion, 1995.

Lois Lowry
All About Sam. Houghton, 1988.
Anastasia Again. Houghton, 1981.
Anastasia at This Address. Houghton, 1991.
Anastasia Has the Answers. Houghton, 1996.
Anastasia Krupnik. Houghton, 1979.
Anastasia On Her Own. Houghton, 1985.
Anastasia Absolutely. Houghton, 1995.
Anastasia Ask Your Analyst. Houghton, 1984.
Attaboy Sam! Houghton, 1992.
Autumn Street. Houghton, 1980.
Gathering Blue, Houghton, 1999.
Giver. Houghton, 1993.
Looking Back. Houghton, 1998.
Number the Stars. Houghton, 1989.
One Hundreth Thing About Caroline. Houghton, 1986.
Rabble Starkey. Houghton, 1987.
See You Around, Sam. Houghton, 1986.
Stay! Houghton, 1997.
Summer to Die. Houghton, 1977.
Switcharound. Houghton, 1985.
Taking Care of Terrific. Houghton, 1983.
Your Move, J.P. Houghton, 1990.
Zooman Sam. Houghton, 1999.

Patricia MacLachlan
All the Places to Love. Harper, 1994.
Arthur, For the Very First Time. Harper, 1989.
Baby. Delacorte. 1995.
Caleb's Story. Harper, 2001.
Cassie Binegar. Harper, 1982.
Facts and Fictions of Minna Pratt. Harper, 1988.
Sarah Plain and Tall. Harper, 1985.
Seven Kisses in a Row. Harper, 1983.
Sick Day. Doubleday, 2001.
Skylark. Harper, 1994.
Three Names. Harper, 1991.
Through Grandpa's Eyes. Harper, 1980.
What You Know First. Harper, 1995.

Scott O'Dell

Black Pearl. Houghton-Mifflin, 1967.
Black Star, Bright Dawn. Houghton-Mifflin, 1988.
Island of the Blue Dolphins. Houghton-Mifflin, 1960.
My Name Is Not Angelica. Houghton-Mifflin, 1989.
Sarah Bishop. Houghton-Mifflin, 1980.
Serpent Never Sleeps. Houghton-Mifflin, 1987.
Sing Down the Moon. Houghton-Mifflin, 1970.
Streams to the River, River to the Sea. Houghton-Mifflin, 1986.
Thunder Rolling in the Mountains. Houghton-Mifflin, 1992.

Katherine Paterson

Bridge to Terabithia. Crowell, 1977.
Come Sing, Jimmy Jo. Lodestar, 1995.
Field of the Dogs. HarperCollins, 2001.
Flip-Flop Girl. Lodestar, 1996.
Great Gilly Hopkins. HarperCollins, 1976.
Jacob Have I Loved. HarperCollins, 1980.
Jip, His Story. Lodestar, 1996.
King's Equal. HarperCollins, 1992.
Lyddie. Lodestar, 1992.
Marvin One Too Many. HarperCollins, 2001.
Marvin's Best Christmas Present Ever. HarperCollins, 1997.
Preacher's Boy. Clarion, 1999.
Same Stuff As Stars. Clarion, 2002.
Zia. Houghton-Mifflin, 1976.

Zilpha Keatley Snyder

Cat Running. Delacorte, 1994.
Egypt Game. Atheneum, 1976.
Gib and the Gray Ghost. Delacorte, 2000.
Gib Rides Home. Delacorte, 1998.
Gypsy Game. Delacorte, 1997.
Headless Cupid. Atheneum, 1983.
Libby On Wednesday. Delacorte, 1991.
Runaways. Delacorte, 1999.
Trespassers. Delacorte, 1995.
Witches of Worm. Atheneum, 1972.

Jerry Spinelli

Bathwater Gang. Little Brown, 1990.
Blue Ribbon Blues. Random House, 1998.
Crash. Knopf, 1996.
Fourth Grade Rats. Scholastic, 1991.
Knots in My Yo-Yo String. Knopf, 1998.
Library Card. Scholastic, 1997.
Maniac Magee. Little Brown, 1990.
Stargirl. Knopf, 1990.

There's A Girl in My Hammerlock. Simon & Schuster, 1993.
Tooter Pepperday. Random House, 1995.
Wringer. HarperCollins, 1997.

Mildred D. Taylor
Friendship. Dial, 1987.
Gold Cadillac. Dial, 1987.
Let the Circle Be Unbroken. Dial, 1981.
Mississippi Bridge. Dial, 1990.
Road to Memphis. Dial, 1990.
Roll of Thunder, Hear My Cry. Dial, 1976.
Song of the Trees. Dial, 1975.
The Well. Dial, 1999.

From *Books Every Child Should Know: The Literature Quiz Book*
by Nancy Polette. Westport, CT: Libraries Unlimited. Copyright © 2006.

NEWBERY QUIZ 1936–2005

1. CADDIE WOODLAWN's mother was upset because she was
   A) a tomboy   B) a girl   C) in poor health

2. The heroine of ROLLER SKATES is named
   A) Lucinda   B) Becky   C) Anne

3. THE WHITE STAG takes place in
   A) Italy   B) England   C) Hungary

4. THIMBLE SUMMER takes place
   A) in a small town   B) on a farm   D) in a girl's school

5. In Daugherty's DANIEL BOONE, before Boone was an explorer he was a
   A) a farmer   B) A Congressman   C) an explorer

6. In CALL IT COURAGE the main character's name is
   A) Lioni   B) Mafatu   C) Brave One

7. In THE MATCHLOCK GUN Edward saves his family from
   A) A bear   B) a fire   C) an Indian attack

8. ADAM OF THE ROAD wandered throughout
   A) England   B) France   C) Scotland

9. JOHNNY TREMAIN injures his
   A) leg   B) hand   C) head

10. In RABBIT HILL the name of the rabbit hit by a car is
    A) Analdas   B) Cottontop   C) Georgie

11. The heroine of STRAWBERRY GIRL is named
    A) Effie   B) Sally   C) Birdie

12. MISS HICKORY is
    A) an old woman   B) a doll   C) a tree

13. THE TWENTY ONE BALLOONS are used to escape from what disaster?
    A) a volcanic eruption B) a flood   C) a terrible fire

14. In KING OF THE WIND, Agba cannot
    A) speak   B) read   C) see

15. In THE DOOR IN THE WALL, Robin wishes to become
    A) king   B) a hunter   C) a knight

continued on next page

NEWBERY QUIZ 1936–2005 (continued)

16. AMOS FORTUNE, FREE MAN begins in what location?

A) Africa   B) United States   C) West Indies

17. In the novel GINGER PYE, Ginger is a

A) gerbil   B) cat   C) dog

18. In SECRET OF THE ANDES a young boy realizes that he wants to be

A) a king   B) a trapper   C) a llama herder

19. AND NOW MIGUEL tells the story of sheepherders in

A) Mexico   B) New Mexico   C) Spain

20. THE WHEEL ON THE SCHOOL takes place in what country?

A) Greece   B) Holland   C) Germany

21. CARRY ON, MR. BOWDITCH tells the story of early

A) navigation   B) steamships   C) submarines

22. In MIRACLES ON MAPLE HILL the children worry about

A) being poor   B) their mother   C) their father

23. RIFLES FOR WATIE takes place during what time in history?

A) Civil War   B) Revolutionary War   C) Spanish-American War

24. The heroine of THE WITCH OF BLACKBIRD POND is named

A) Mary   B) Sarah   C) Kit

25. In ONION JOHN the townspeople give him

A) a house   B) money   C) food

26. In ISLAND OF THE BLUE DOLPHINS Karana's brother is killed by

A) sharks   B) savage dogs   C) a bear

27. In THE BRONZE BOW Daniel is consumed with hatred for

A) the British   B) the Greeks   C) the Romans

28. In A WRINKLE IN TIME Meg's mother is a

A) teacher   B) a scientist   C) a doctor

29. IT'S LIKE THIS, CAT takes place in what city?

A) New York   B) Boston   C) New Orleans

30. In SHADOW OF A BULL the boy who does not want to be a bullfighter is

A) Carlos   B) Jose   C) Manolo

31. The main character in I, JUAN DE PAREJA is

A)   a slave   B) a musician   C) a scientist

continued on next page

From *Books Every Child Should Know: The Literature Quiz Book*
by Nancy Polette. Westport, CT: Libraries Unlimited. Copyright © 2006.

NEWBERY QUIZ 1936–2005 (continued)

32. In UP A ROAD SLOWLY, Julie finds it difficult to live with

    A) her grandfather   B) her aunt   C) her stepmother

33. The children in THE MIXED UP FILES run away and hide in

    A) a firehouse   B) a deserted school   C) a museum

34. THE HIGH KING'S first job was that of a

    A) knight   B) pigkeeper   C) page

35. In SOUNDER a boy searches for his father who is

    A) in a mental hospital   B) in prison   C) in the army

36. SUMMER OF THE SWANS is about a missing

    A) boy   B) dog   C) ring

37. MRS. FRISBY is a

    A) woman   B) mouse   C) nosey neighbor

38. In JULIE OF THE WOLVES Julie has a pen pal in what state?

    A) New Mexico   B) Arizona   C) California

39. THE SLAVE DANCER takes place

    A) on a plantation   B) in an African village C) on a ship

40. M.C. HIGGINS, THE GREAT is a

    A) magician   B) 13-year-old boy   C) famous actor

41. In THE GREY KING, it is Will Stanton's destiny to find

    A) his family   B) a harp   C) a sword

42. ROLL OF THUNDER, HEAR MY CRY takes place in what time period?

    A) the Depression years   B) World War One   C) Civil War

43. In BRIDGE OF TERABITHIA a child must cope with the loss of

    A) his mother   B) a friend   C) his dog

44. The goal of THE WESTING GAME is to receive

    A) a job   B) an inheritance   C) one hundred dollars

45. In A GATHERING OF DAYS a 14-year-old girl writes of her father's

    A) illness   B) job   C) remarriage

46. In JACOB HAVE I LOVED, a young girl feels she cannot compete with

    A) her classmates   B) her sister   C) her brother

continued on next page

From *Books Every Child Should Know: The Literature Quiz Book*
by Nancy Polette. Westport, CT: Libraries Unlimited. Copyright © 2006.

NEWBERY QUIZ 1936–2005 (continued)

47. The Inn in A VISIT TO WILLIAM BLAKE'S INN is

    A) run down   B) imaginary   C) located in Ireland

48. At the beginning of DICEY'S SONG, where is Dicey's mother?

    A) in prison   B) in a mental institution   C) in the hospital

49. Mr. Henshaw in DEAR MR. HENSHAW is

    A) a writer   B) a minister   C) a teacher

50. The dragonkiller in THE HERO AND THE CROWN is named

    A) Aerin   B) Damar   C) Una

51. SARAH, PLAIN AND TALL misses

    A) her brother   B) the sea   C) the mountains

52. In THE WHIPPING BOY Jemmy and Prince Brat are chased through the London

    A) sewers   B) streets   C) alleys

53. The award for LINCOLN, A PHOTOBIOGRAPHY was won by

    A) Scott O'Dell   B) Russell Freedman   C) Tom Brokaw

54. JOYFUL NOISE is a series of poems for

    A) insects   B) bats   C) spiders

55. NUMBER THE STARS takes place during what war?

    A) World War Two   B) World War One   C) Civil War

56. MANIAC MAGEE was orphaned at the age of

    A) twelve   B) six   C) three

57. SHILOH is the story of a boy and a

    A) girl   B) dog   C) cat

58. In MISSING MAY, May is what relation to the main character?

    A) her mother   B) her aunt   C) her grandmother

59. In THE GIVER, what does the giver give?

    A) memories   B) money   C) happiness

60. At the end of WALK TWO MOONS a girl finds her mother's

    A) grave   B) ring   C) diary

61. The name of the MIDWIFE'S APPRENTICE was

    A) Alice   B) Sarah   C) Sally

continued on next page

NEWBERY QUIZ 1936–2005 (continued)

62. THE VIEW FROM SATURDAY is about a sixth grade

   A) class party　　　　B) Academic Bowl Team　　C) camping trip

63. OUT OF THE DUST takes place on a wheat farm in

   A) Minnesota　　　　B) Oklahoma　　　　C) Iowa

64. The names of two boys in HOLES are

   A) Stanley and XRay　　B) Loser and Chuck　　C) NoGood and Rapper

65. In BUD, NOT BUDDY what does Herman E. Calloway do for a living?

   A) salesman　　　　B) lawyer　　　　C) musician

66. Who do the children visit in A YEAR DOWN YONDER?

   A) aunt　　　　B) good friends　　　　C) grandmother

67. In what country does A SINGLE SHARD take place ?

   A) China　　　　B) Korea　　　　C) Japan

68. CRISPEN: THE CROSS OF LEAD takes place during what century and in what country?

   A) 12th-century France　　B) 20th-century Ireland　　C) 14th-century England

69. In THE TALE OF DESPEREAUX who is Despereaux?

   A) a French boy　　　　B) a mouse　　　　C) an old man

70. In KIRA KIRA the parents find work in

   A) a factory　　　B) a chicken processing plant　　C) a laundry

Key: 1. A 2. A 3. C 4. B 5. A 6. B 7. C 8. A 9. B 10. C 11. C 12. B 13. A 14. A 15. C 16. A 17. C 18. C 19. B 20. B 21. A 22. C 23. A 24. C 25. A 26. B 27. C 28. B 29. A 30. C 31. A 32. B 33. C 34. B 35. B 36. B 37. B 38. C 39. C 40. B 41. B 42. A 43. B 44. B 45. C 46. B 47. B 48. B 49. A 50. A 51. B 52. A 53. B 54. A 55. A 56. C 57. B 58. B 59. A 60. A 61. A 62. B 63. B 64. A 65. C 66. C 67. B 68. C 69. B 70. B

NEWBERY MEDAL WINNERS

2005: *Kira-Kira* by Cynthia Kadohata. New York, Atheneum

2004: *The Tale of Despereaux: Being the Story of a Mouse, a Princess, Some Soup, and a Spool of Thread* by Kate DiCamillo. New York, Candlewick Press

2003: *Crispin: The Cross of Lead* by Avi. New York, Hyperion Books for Children

2002: *A Single Shard* by Linda Sue Park. New York, Clarion Books/Houghton Mifflin

2001: *A Year Down Yonder* by Richard Peck. New York, Dial

2000: *Bud, Not Buddy* by Christopher Paul Curtis. New York, Delacorte

1999: *Holes* by Louis Sachar. New York, Frances Foster Books

1998: *Out of the Dust* by Karen Hesse. New York, Scholastic

1997: *The View from Saturday* by E.L. Konigsburg. New York, Jean Karl/ Atheneum

1996: *The Midwife's Apprentice* by Karen Cushman. New York, Clarion

1995: *Walk Two Moons* by Sharon Creech. New York, HarperCollins

1994: *The Giver* by Lois Lowry. Boston, Houghton Mifflin

1993: *Missing May* by Cynthia Rylant. New York, Jackson/Orchard

1992: *Shiloh* by Phyllis Reynolds Naylor. New York, Atheneum

1991: *Maniac Magee* by Jerry Spinelli. New York, Little, Brown

1990: *Number the Stars* by Lois Lowry. Boston, Houghton Mifflin

1989: *Joyful Noise: Poems for Two Voices* by Paul Fleischman. New York, Harper& Row

1988: *Lincoln: A Photobiography* by Russell Freedman. New York, Clarion

1987: *The Whipping Boy* by Sid Fleischman. New York, Greenwillow

1986: *Sarah, Plain and Tall* by Patricia MacLachlan. New York, HarperCollins

1985: *The Hero and the Crown* by Robin McKinley. New York, Greenwillow

1984: *Dear Mr. Henshaw* by Beverly Cleary. New York, Morrow

1983: *Dicey's Song* by Cynthia Voigt. New York, Atheneum

1982: *A Visit to William Blake's Inn: Poems for Innocent and Experienced Travelers* by Nancy Willard. New York, Harcourt

1981: *Jacob Have I Loved* by Katherine Paterson. New York, Crowell

1980: *A Gathering of Days: A New England Girl's Journal, 1830–1832* by Joan W. Blos. New York, Scribner

1979: *The Westing Game* by Ellen Raskin. New York, Dutton

1978: *Bridge to Terabithia* by Katherine Paterson. New York, Crowell

1977: *Roll of Thunder, Hear My Cry* by Mildred D. Taylor. New York, Dial

From *Books Every Child Should Know: The Literature Quiz Book*
by Nancy Polette. Westport, CT: Libraries Unlimited. Copyright © 2006.

1976: *The Grey King* by Susan Cooper. New York, McElderry/Atheneum

1975: *M. C. Higgins, the Great* by Virginia Hamilton. New York, Macmillan

1974: *The Slave Dancer* by Paula Fox. New York, Bradbury

1973: *Julie of the Wolves* by Jean Craighead George. New York, Harper & Row

1972: *Mrs. Frisby and the Rats of NIMH* by Robert C. O'Brien. New York, Atheneum

1971: *Summer of the Swans* by Betsy Byars. New York, Viking

1970: *Sounder* by William H. Armstrong. New York, Harper & Row

1969: *The High King* by Lloyd Alexander. New York, Holt Rinehart & Winston

1968: *From the Mixed-Up Files of Mrs. Basil E. Frankweiler* by E.L. Konigsberg. New York, Atheneum

1967: *Up A Road Slowly* by Irene Hunt. Chicago, Follett

1966: *I, Juan de Pareja* by Elizabeth Borton de Trivino. New York, Farrar

1965: *Shadow of a Bull* by Maia Wojciechowska. New York, Atheneum

1964: *It's Like This, Cat* by Emily Neville. New York, Harper & Row

1963: *A Wrinkle in Time* by Madeleine L'Engle. New York, Farrar, Straus & Giroux

1962: *The Bronze Bow* by Elizabeth George Speare. Boston, Houghton Mifflin

1961: *Island of the Blue Dolphins* by Scott O'Dell. Boston, Houghton Mifflin

1960: *Onion John* by Joseph Krumgold. New York, Thomas Y. Crowell

1959: *The Witch of Blackbird Pond* by Elizabeth George Speare. Boston, Houghton Mifflin

1958: *Rifles for Watie* by Harold Keith. New York, Thomas Y. Crowell

1957: *Miracles on Maple Hill* by Virginia Sorenson. New York, Harcourt Brace

1956: *Carry On, Mr. Bowditch* by Jean Lee Latham. Boston, Houghton Mifflin

1955: *The Wheel on the School* by Meindert DeJong. New York, Harper & Row

1954: *. . . And Now Miguel* by Joseph Krumgold. New York, Thomas Y. Crowell

1953: *Secret of the Andes* by Ann Nolan Clark. New York, Viking

1952: *Ginger Pye* by Eleanor Estes. New York, Harcourt Brace

1951: *Amos Fortune, Free Man* by Elizabeth Yates. New York, E. P. Dutton

1950: *The Door in the Wall* by Marguerite de Angeli. New York, Doubleday

1949: *King of the Wind* by Marguerite Henry. Chicago, Rand McNally

1948: *The Twenty-One Balloons* by William Pène du Bois. New York, Viking

1947: *Miss Hickory* by Carolyn Sherwin Bailey. New York, Viking

1946: *Strawberry Girl* by Lois Lenski. New York, Lippincott

1945: *Rabbit Hill* by Robert Lawson. New York, Viking

From *Books Every Child Should Know: The Literature Quiz Book* by Nancy Polette. Westport, CT: Libraries Unlimited. Copyright © 2006.

1944:   *Johnny Tremain* by Esther Forbes. Boston, Houghton Mifflin

1943:   *Adam of the Road* by Elizabeth Janet Gray. New York, Viking

1942:   *The Matchlock Gun* by Walter Edmonds. Indianapolis, Dodd Mead

1941:   *Call It Courage* by Armstrong Sperry. New York, Macmillan

1940:   *Daniel Boone* by James Daugherty. New York, Viking

1939:   *Thimble Summer* by Elizabeth Enright. New York, Rinehart

1938:   *The White Stag* by Kate Seredy. New York, Viking

1937:   *Roller Skates* by Ruth Sawyer. New York, Viking

1936:   *Caddie Woodlawn* by Carol Ryrie Brink. New York, Macmillan

1935:   *Dobry* by Monica Shannon. New York, Viking

1934:   *Invincible Louisa: The Story of the Author of Little Women* by Cornelia Meigs. New York, Little, Brown

1933:   *Young Fu of the Upper Yangtze* by Elizabeth Lewis. New York, Winston

1932:   *Waterless Mountain* by Laura Adams Armer. New York, Longmans

1931:   *The Cat Who Went to Heaven* by Elizabeth Coatsworth. New York, Macmillan

1930:   *Hitty, Her First Hundred Years* by Rachel Field. New York, Macmillan

1929:   *The Trumpeter of Krakow* by Eric P. Kelly. New York, Macmillan

1928:   *Gay Neck, the Story of a Pigeon* by Dhan Gopal Mukerji. New York, E.P. Dutton

1927:   *Smoky, the Cowhorse* by Will James. New York, Scribner

1926:   *Shen of the Sea* by Arthur Bowie Chrisman. New York, E.P. Dutton

1925:   *Tales from Silver Lands* by Charles Finger. New York, Doubleday

1924:   *The Dark Frigate* by Charles Hawes. New York, Little, Brown

1923:   *The Voyages of Doctor Dolittle* by Hugh Lofting. New York, Lippincott

1922:   *The Story of Mankind* by Hendrik Willem van Loon. New York, Liveright

From *Books Every Child Should Know: The Literature Quiz Book*
by Nancy Polette. Westport, CT: Libraries Unlimited. Copyright © 2006.

ABOUT THE AUTHOR

NANCY POLETTE is an educator with over 30 years experience. She has authored over 150 professional titles. She lives and works in O'Fallon, Missouri, where she is a professor at Lindenwood College.